BEYOND
THE DOG'S NOSE

To Teddy from

From

Mother

June, 19 — 1934.

THE BOYS AND UNCLE EB AND TINY THUMB CLIMBED ABOUT THE
MAZE OF CHESTS AND TREASURE

[*page* 189]

BEYOND THE DOG'S NOSE

BY
HAROLD M. SHERMAN
("EDWARD J. MORROW")

AUTHOR OF
GET 'EM MAYFIELD, MAYFIELD'S
FIGHTING FIVE, ETC.

GROSSET & DUNLAP
PUBLISHERS   NEW YORK

TO

THOMAS HENRY SHERMAN

MY FATHER

WHO GAVE ME THE IDEA UPON WHICH THIS
ADVENTURE STORY IS FOUNDED AND
WHO, SINCE, HAS ENTERED UPON THE
ADVENTURE OF THE GREAT BEYOND.
HIM I SALUTE WITH LASTING
ADMIRATION AND AFFECTION!

CONTENTS

CHAPTER I

THINGS BEGIN TO HAPPEN

"WELL, fellows—here we are!" announced Giggles Hungerford, unslinging his pack with an air of relief. "Pretty good time we made, too. An hour and three-quarters on the hike isn't bad for seven miles over rough country."

"Humph! We'd have made it in less than that if we hadn't stopped to take a look at the winter quarters of Brockton's World's Greatest Shows," sniffed Bing Miller disdainfully.

"Some winter quarters, believe me!" echoed Curly Lamb, straddling the low fence by the clearing. "Nothing there but a sick lion and a quill-less porcupine!"

"What can you expect in the dead of summer?" retorted Giggles. "The show doesn't make any money leaving its menagerie behind. You're lucky to have seen a sick lion. I told you the place wasn't worth making that detour for!"

"Well, Curly'd never been satisfied if we hadn't," kidded Bing. "It's a wonder he hasn't run off and joined a circus long ago. I can see him in a side show now—billed as the Freckled Wonder—more freckles per square inch than any other human being alive. Freckles absolutely guaranteed not to rub off. . . ."

"Oh, dry up!" ordered Curly. "You're not so far from a freak yourself—the world's longest string bean—with legs so long it takes him fifteen minutes to get his trousers on!"

"Tee, hee, hee!" giggled Giggles. "I'm glad there's nothing queer about me. . . ."

"Queer about you . . . !"

"Say, you're the queerest one of the lot!"

"Why, how do you make that out?" The leader of the trio registered a look of rare innocence and surprise.

"The boy with the . . ." started Bing.

"Hyena's laugh!" finished Curly.

Giggles gazed from one chum to the other, mirthfully.

"You're just jealous," he said, "that's all that's the matter with you. Now if either one of you birds had my laugh, you'd have something!"

"Yeah," accepted Bing, drily, "a jail sentence probably. You're the only person I know of that could get away with a laugh like that in a civilized community!"

"Come on, let's cut out the choice compliments and get down to camping," invited Giggles. "We've a tent to put up, a fire to build, and lots of other things, before it gets dark!"

"Gee, did old Uncle Eb really say we could pitch camp here?" asked Curly, unbelievingly.

"He sure did!"

"Why, it's right in sight of his funny old house," continued Curly, peering through the trees. "Say, that house is so close to the edge of the bluff it looks like anybody could stand on the other side and push it plump into Lake Michigan!"

Bing and Giggles paused in their labors of unpacking to follow Curly's gaze.

"I don't see why it was ever built so close," pondered Giggles, thoughtfully. "Just to be different, I s'pose. Then, Uncle Eb's grandfather—that's old Ebenezer Beecher—was a sailor; and he probably wanted to be where he could look out over the lake whenever he took a notion."

"Huh! The house ought to suit Uncle Eb just as well," ruminated Bing. "He was a sailor, too. . . . I'll bet he spends most of his time sitting in there . . . staring at the lake. . . ."

"Oh, I don't know," objected Curly.

"Well, what else would there be for him to do?" demanded Bing. "You seldom see him outside the place. He only goes to town twice a month to get provisions, and he doesn't speak to anybody there but Hank Dawson, the storekeeper—or Doc Russell—if he sees him—or our friend, Giggles, here. . . ."

Giggles patted himself on the chest importantly. "I'm some guy, I am!"

"Some *lucky* guy," modified Curly. "If you hadn't happened to be going past Uncle Eb's place

3

last winter when he was sick and needed help . . . he wouldn't have paid any attention to you either!"

"And you wouldn't have had the chance to see what his crazy house looked like inside," added Bing. "Just think—Doc Russell and you are the only two living persons, so far as any one knows, who've ever crossed old Uncle Eb's doorsill!"

"What's the place look like?" asked Curly with fresh eagerness, taking another glance at the house.

"Aw, say, I've told you all about it a million times! There wasn't much to see except bare walls and a few pieces of home-made furniture. And besides, I didn't get to go through more than three rooms. Trust Uncle Eb for that! He may have been on his deathbed for all he knew but he wasn't going to permit any sight-seeing trips on his premises. No, siree! Doc Russell started for the back part of the house once and old Uncle Eb took on such a coughing fit that the Doc turned right around and came back. I don't know what the Doc thought about it, but it just came to me that Uncle Eb had coughed like that on purpose."

"Well, gee!" wondered Bing, spreading out the tent canvas. "What's the old geezer trying to keep under cover anyway?"

"Search me," laughed Giggles, shrugging his shoulders and laying hold of the tent. "Why would he sit for hours out on his front stoop with a loaded shotgun across his knees?"

4

"Maybe it's to scare away mosquitoes," suggested Curly, ducking quickly to avoid being hit.

"There's no use talking. . . . Uncle Eb's got several good-sized bats in his belfry," declared Giggles, "but he's not as dangerous as he looks. He's got his good side, too. Treat him right and he treats you right. Witness his letting us camp on his property! You fellows thought I was nutty for even thinking of asking him, didn't you? Well, nobody could have been nicer. He even seemed glad to figure on our coming, and suggested this very spot for us to pitch camp!"

The three chums looked out over the bluff to the west, and toward Lake Michigan which stretched out and out and blended with the horizon a thin, hazy line that the late afternoon sun was slipping down behind.

"It's a great spot all right!" agreed Curly, enthusiastically. "Think of being three hundred feet above Lake Michigan, on a sheer bluff! Hear those waves washing . . . and washing . . . against the rock wall below. Won't it be fun, digging into our sleeping bags and lying awake, looking out under the flaps of the tent, watching for the lights of freighters and passenger steamers—miles out—and listening to the swish swash of that water . . . !

"And thinking of Uncle Eb, sitting in his great big house, all alone, watching, too," reminded Bing, driving a tent stake.

The boys worked in silence a few moments as the sun dipped into the lake, throwing a shadow over the bluff.

"Say," said Curly, impulsively, "it's just beginning to dawn on me what a lonely existence old Uncle Eb must lead! There's something about this place that would give me the creeps if it wasn't for you two fellows being with me. I wouldn't want to spend a night up here all by myself. Not for half the earth! And Uncle Eb has lived there, in that house that his grandfather left him, for years!"

"Not alone, though," corrected Bing. "Have you forgot his little dog, Spot?"

"Humph!" snorted Curly, "I've seen times when a dog wouldn't be any company!"

"See here, you guys!" censured Giggles, "it's going to be dark and we're not going to be half finished. *Can* Uncle Eb for a few minutes. You'll get enough of him before we're through here. He'll probably be over to-night to see how we're fixed, and if I don't miss a good guess, I'll bet he trots out all his pet hallucinations for our edification and enjoyment!"

"I surrender," gasped Bing, "I thought anything over three syllable words was barred in this league!"

Realizing that there was much to do and that they had taken up considerable time in idle talking, the boys hurried up their work and just managed to get their more important tasks completed as the sun disappeared entirely, leaving a radiant glimmer

6

over the lake which gradually shimmered out into a dusky hue.

Giggles, Bing and Curly had left the little town of Bean Blossom, seven miles distant, intending to be gone a week. There was more than the ordinary interest among townspeople who knew of their prospective camping trip for the reason that the boys were to invade Uncle Eb's "sacred territory," as his property was called. Heretofore no one had so much as thought of putting a foot upon Uncle Eb's premises, except in the instance of Giggles' being hailed by the grizzled-faced old man and invited in. To attempt to trespass without permission was courting several kinds of quick disaster in the opinion of those who knew Uncle Eb and his peculiar kinks. "A good person to steer clear of" was frequent advice handed out to the younger element of Bean Blossom, it being generally agreed that Uncle Eb was perfectly harmless only in so far as he was not molested. Old settlers recognized in him an old codger who was plagued with wild hallucinations. They could recall times when he had recited, with actual terror, of how there were certain people who were trying to "get him"; that there was something in his fortress-like mansion that somebody wanted. In days gone by a few Bean Blossom citizens had investigated Uncle Eb's fanciful stories, nothing ever coming of these investigations but a stronger conviction that poor Uncle Eb was "cracked," or "was not all there." Now no one could be found who

7

would pay any attention to the eccentric character and Uncle Eb, seeming to sense this aloofness and disbelief in his tales, had practically silenced his tongue. "Like grandfather, like grandson," might have been an epithet to have applied here, for Uncle Eb had certainly followed directly in old Ebenezer Beecher's footsteps. And old Ebenezer Beecher, according to the vague recollection of Max Arms, Bean Blossom's oldest inhabitant, had been a character of characters! Why, he had been rumored to have shot a man just because the individual had dared speak to him! A salty salt, a big-chested, queer-acting six-footer, Ebenezer Beecher had come to Bean Blossom, then but sparsely settled, and had caused his house to be built. But, instead of calling upon the settlers round about to help build it, he had brought workmen with him aboard a sailing vessel! And, once built, Ebenezer Beecher had locked the forbidding looking house up, and embarked once more upon the lake, giving fair warning, however, that if the house wasn't found exactly as he had left it when he returned, he'd shoot every settler on sight. Cheerful tidings! But how his threat worked! Every settler, to protect himself, had seen to it that his neighbor had kept away from the mansion on the bluffs. Nothing much was known about old Ebenezer Beecher except that he was a man of his word. On top of that Ebenezer seemed to stand in well with the Indians. And that part of Michigan, in those days, was not free from the possibility of violence. It was quite evident, from the lake captain's actions, that all he desired was to be left entirely alone, and this the settlers gladly decided to do, so long as Ebenezer, in turn, respected their rights.

For more than thirty years, Ebenezer and his sailing vessel came and went . . . at irregular intervals. No one had ever been seen about the premises in the daytime but occasionally, at night, lights had been seen moving about inside the house. Settlers, seeing, shook their heads forebodingly, but discreetly refrained from inquiry. It was Ebenezer's doings, not theirs. And then came a time when Ebenezer and his sailing vessel were gone longer than usual; a time when, the settlers hoped, some dire calamity had overtaken their ruthless neighbor. A day later a new face put in appearance, a younger face, a stalwart body, though shorter and thicker set, but a head crowned with the same pointed sailor's hat! Settlers had wondered then . . . and a few had bolstered up nerve to make advances . . . and finally to ask questions. But their boldness and curiosity had profited them nothing, for the stranger had proven as cold and unfeeling as Ebenezer Beecher himself, as though he had gone to school under Ebenezer . . . and had been taught or had pounded into him, Ebenezer's frigid conduct. What the settlers subsequently learned, came only through surmising; but it was definitely established finally that the new guardian of the house on the bluff was

9

a direct descendant of old Ebenezer Beecher—a grandson, in fact; and that something had happened to the hardened old grandfather. Years of residence in the mansion erected by his forebear had won for the new occupant the title of Uncle Eb. Thus is one acquainted with all that was known of the past concerning these two strange, hermit-like men.

"Oh, boy! What do you think of my camp fire?" demanded Bing, standing back from the licking tongues of flame which leaped skyward. "I'll bet they can see that as far as Chicago anyway!"

"Go on, Chicago isn't on Lake Michigan," kidded Curly.

"It is in my geography," rejoined Bing, unaffected. "Remember, years ago, when the big Chicago fire took place?"

"No—and you don't either!"

"Well, er—a—I mean, remember hearing tell about how the smoke from that big confla—"

"Look out for any words above three syllables!" warned Giggles.

". . . bonfire," substituted Bing.

"Some bonfire all right," agreed Curly. "What about it?"

"Why . . . well . . . I was going to say . . ." stammered Bing, mixed up. "Say, if you guys didn't break in with so many interr—"

"Three syllables!" warned Curly.

"With so many . . . so many . . ." groped Bing, desperately. "Oh, hang the three syllable league!"

Giggles and Curly enjoyed a good laugh.

"What I'm really driving at is that if a little spontaneous combustion like a cow kicking over a lamp in a woodshed in Chicago should have started a conflagration sufficient to scatter smoke the length of Lake Michigan so dense as to be almost impenetrable . . ." Bing stopped for breath.

"Yes, yes, go on!" encouraged Giggles.

". . . it is then easily conceivable and entirely comprehensible," resumed Bing, "how a master fire builder like myself can, without the aid of a cow . . ."

". . . or a bucket of milk . . ."

". . . or a three-legged stool . . ."

Suggestions from the audience!

". . . build a fire of much more far-reaching import," continued Bing, undaunted. "Because, ladies and gentlemen, my fire is builded upon one of the greatest and most widely used foundations of to-day . . . it is builded upon a *bluff!*"

"Yeow!"

"Stone him!"

"He can't bluff us. In the lake for that, the first thing in the morning! Before the sun's up, when it's nice and cold!"

There is no telling what might have happened to one Bing Miller but for the happening of something else which took the minds of all three boys off their joshing.

"Hold on!" cried Giggles, suddenly. "Did you see that flash?"

"Should say I did!" exclaimed Curly. "What do you suppose it was?"

"It seemed to come right up over the bluff here!" said Bing, feeling his way to the edge and looking over. "Gee, it was bright, wasn't it?" He drew back his head quickly. "Wow—there it is again!"

"Tee, hee, hee!" giggled Giggles.

"Shut up!" commanded Bing, nervously.

"C-c-can't a fellow laugh if he wants to?" asked Giggles, peering down into the darkness from whence the strange flash had come.

"Yeah . . . when there's something to laugh at," retorted Curly. "I told you this place gave me the creeps!"

"Say, you're not letting a little thing like a flash of light scare you, are you?"

"N-no . . . I'm just wondering how a flash of light could be coming from down there, that's all. There's no shore line down there at all, you *know* that. And the water pounds up against this bluff, about fifty feet deep!"

"Don't some fish have lights?" persisted Giggles.

"Maybe it was the back fire from my bonfire," suggested Bing, dryly. "Something had to cause it, that's sure. It looked to me like some one taking a flashlight picture. Funny . . . not a sound of any kind!"

"The aurora borealis!" deduced Curly, not to be outdone.

Giggles and Bing registered disgust.

"No kidding," said Giggles, "that's the queerest thing I've seen in a long time. You were nearest the edge, Bing. Could you see where the light appeared to come from?"

Bing shook his head. The three chums examined each other's faces, which seemed to dance in the flickering light of their fire. The three were between the fire and the precipitous edge of the great cliff. Behind them yawned the darkness, now pitch black. In front of them stretched space—black, dropping space—and the water, splashing against the marblelike wall below.

"The flash didn't seem to have any starting place," explained Bing. "It just spread out, near the water, and lighted up."

"Did you see anything that looked like a boat . . . or . . . or anything?" asked Curly.

"No," answered Bing, with certainty.

A noise by the fire startled them. The boys swung about quickly; then caught their breaths and all but cried out.

Standing on the opposite side of the fire and gazing at them through the smoky heat waves was the figure of a man. A bewhiskered face stretched in a leering smile; eyes which looked unusually white and

13

protruding; a shabby, pointed sailor's cap; a torn blouse and jumpers; gnarled hands on hips. Uncle Eb, to be sure. More like Uncle Eb's ghost.

"Bow-wow-wow! Bow-wow-wow!"

And Spot, too, dancing around the fire, his stub of a tail sticking up defiantly, ears back, ready for battle. Not any more sociable than Uncle Eb, in fact, not nearly as sociable as Uncle Eb appeared to be now.

"Spot!" rasped the lone occupant of the strange house on the bluff. Spot whimpered and retreated to his master, crawling along on his belly to lick Uncle Eb's roughened shoe tops.

"Well, boys, did you see it?" asked the man who had given them permission to camp on his property. There was a note of almost savage joy in his question. Giggles, Bing and Curly felt their scalps tingle uncomfortably. They came back toward Uncle Eb and the fire.

"See what?" asked Giggles, suspiciously.

Uncle Eb grinned wisely and lifted a ragged sleeve to motion toward the lake.

"The light," he said, simply.

Giggles glanced at his two chums consultingly. Here was something that they certainly could not attribute to Uncle Eb's hallucinations. This had actually happened. Or, if it hadn't, they were bughouse too. Giggles gulped.

"Yes, we saw it," he nodded, "what was it?"

Uncle Eb laughed, a cackling laugh . . . a laugh

14

enough to send a chill racing up and down spines.

"So—you *saw* it!" he said, finally. "With your own eyes, not *my* eyes, *your* eyes! And they say Uncle Eb is crazy! Ask me what it is! Ask me is the North Star inhabited! I calls it the 'spirit light.' It always comes before things happen. It means Uncle Eb is in for a bad night again, Uncle Eb will see devilish things, and folks will say there is nobody home." The old grandson of old grandfather Ebenezer Beecher tapped his head significantly. "But this time, Mister Giggles here, and his two friends, they see for themselves, and they say, 'there *is* somebody home. Uncle Eb's no fool, he's a brave man, a *very brave* man.' Ain't that so, Spot?"

Spot resumed his licking of his master's shoes.

Giggles, Bing and Curly stood silently, casting anxious glances about them into the darkness. Before coming to this place to camp, they had been intrigued by the thought of adventure which sojourning on Uncle Eb's property had suggested, but, right at this moment, it is quite probable that each of the three would have traded everything he owned if he could have been picked up and set down in some far distant locality. The impression was now firmly implanted in their minds that this vicinity was not exactly healthy; it gave promise of breeding all sorts of weird things; and hearing Uncle Eb talk about it didn't help matters any, either.

"M-M-Maybe we'd better not camp here after all," suggested Bing, tremulously, wondering how long it would take him to reach Bean Blossom if he dogtrotted all the way home.

The owner of the property grinned cordially.

"Now don't let me be scarin' you," he reassured, "them 'spirit lights' ain't nothin'. They always stay right there, over the bluff. But it's the headless men, and swords slashin' through the air without any hands to 'em, and human yells comin' from where no human bein's is—them's the things that makes a body a little mite uneasy!"

"Gee, this is no place for us!" whispered Curly, pulling at Bing's arm.

"Tee, hee, hee!" giggled Giggles. "How interesting!"

Uncle Eb gazed at the giggler curiously.

"He thinks you're kidding him," informed Bing, looking daggers at Giggles. Then, in an undertone, "Hey, what's the grand idea? You'll have us invited to spend the night inside his house next!"

"Well, isn't that what you'd like?" replied Giggles, in a low voice. "You've always been wondering how it looked—here's your chance!"

Giggles was gripped compellingly from both sides.

"Kiddin' you!" scorned Uncle Eb, taking a step closer and shoving his grizzled face forward until the eyes seemed to catch some of the blaze from the fire. "Say, if I'd begin to tell you boys what I've

16

seen, and heard, and been through the past six months—well—you'd turn tail and run so fast you'd not get caught up to yourselves in a week! But I'm not goin' to say a thing. I'm goin' to let you find out for yourselves. They's somebody tryin' to 'get' old Uncle Eb. They's somethin' he's got that they wants. And they's not goin' to be satisfied till they gets it. But Uncle Eb's a better man than they be! He knows how to defend his house, he does! They's gotten in many times . . . but he's druv them out. Uncle Eb's a brave man—a very brave man. Eh, Spot?"

Spot did not lick his master's shoes this time. He merely wagged his tail. The lone occupant of the house on the bluff laughed his cackling laugh.

"Spot always agrees with me," he said. "Always . . . always! He's a brave dog—a very brave dog —it takes a very brave dog to live with a very brave man. How're you boys fixed for the night?"

Uncle Eb's mind seemed to be rambling. He blinked as he peered around at the tent, back in the shadows cast by the fire.

"We're . . . we're fixed fine, thanks," responded Giggles.

"That's good," answered the property owner, evidently pleased. "Better keep a fire burnin' all night, though," he added, "I always keep a lamp lit at the house. It makes it harder for anythin' to get you!"

Giggles, Bing and Curly exchanged startled, wondering glances.

"Well, Spot . . . we'd better be gettin' back to the house before the devilment starts, don't you think?"

Spot did, with several "Bow-wows."

"But you haven't any light to guide you!" protested Giggles. "Here, let us lend you one of our flashlights. You'll never see your way through that thicket, and those trees!"

"*Won't* I?" chuckled Uncle Eb. "Say, son, I could walk along the very edge of that cliff and never make a misstep. I know every blade of grass, and shrub, and tree, and rock on these here premises— and they all gets out of the way when they feel me comin'! Besides, I never carry a light nights for *personal* reasons. In the house it's different. I want 'em to know I'm there."

"WHO?" asked Giggles, impulsively.

But Uncle Eb's cackling laugh was the only answer. He had shambled off, the darkness swallowing him up almost immediately. For ten long, pulsating minutes the three chums stood, hands on each other's shoulders, straining their eyes in the direction of Uncle Eb's house, no one speaking. Then, finally, the tiniest gleam appeared, growing boldly into a flickering light.

"Ah!" the chums exclaimed together, relieved.

Bing turned accusingly to Giggles.

"So you were the one who thought it would be so

much fun to camp on Uncle Eb's property! A nice, restful place, no one to bother us, great view of Lake Michigan, lots of wild country around us . . . bah!"

"Two bahs!" echoed Curly.

"Make it a whole flock of sheep!" sided in Giggles, "I admit it looks like we're going to get more than we'd bargained for. But why should *we* kick? It isn't often that folks get more than their money's worth nowadays."

"I don't want more than my money's worth," objected Bing, "I'm more than satisfied right now."

"Say, you're not going back to Bean Blossom just because you saw a funny light you couldn't understand and heard an old man tell you funny stories about headless heads and swordless swords . . . ."

"Headless heads? Swordless swords?"

"Well, whatever they were . . . ," corrected Giggles. "For my part I'm mighty glad we're here. I hope something *does* happen. Maybe we can figure out what it's all about and set Uncle Eb's mind at ease. I'll bet he's gotten all worked up over some very simple cause—something that could be explained in a jiffy if a person just went after things right."

"No doubt," said Curly, skeptically.

"I'm curious about that light," insisted Giggles. "Just think, we've got a whole week ahead of us to find out what caused it! To-morrow morning, when it's so we can see, we'll examine the face of the cliff.

Right at present I'm rather tired. I move we bank our fire and turn in."

"Second the motion," said Bing, after a moment's consideration.

So the fire was banked, Curly proving a silent helper. But it was at least two hours after they had retired before all three could settle down enough to drop to sleep. And even then, Giggles at Bing's insistence had lain down with his thirty-two rifle within easy reach. Bing and Curly had each a sharp-edged hatchet and some skinning knives—these weapons in addition to flashlights which might be grabbed up on the shortest of notice. No, the boys were not unduly alarmed, but none of them had taken off their clothes! Chances were nothing would happen, but, if it did . . . ?

Being asleep the boys were not aware of a remarkably small figure which crept stealthily—oh, so stealthily—up to the flap of the tent and peered in, and grinned from ear to ear, and crept away and reported to some other figures hiding in the thicket.

"Only kids!" the figure said, and the other figures had laughed softly, and started toward the house on the bluff.

But, an hour later, yes, a good hour . . . the three sleepers came suddenly awake with goose pimples oozing out all over them. They raised up on elbows, listening, and as they listened their blood began to pump madly through their veins.

"Ow . . . oooooh! Ow . . . oooooh!" sounded

the most uncanny of yells, a wavering sort of yell. And then, almost on top of it, a piercing scream which they instantly recognized as coming from old Uncle Eb!

Bang! Bang!

Giggles, Bing and Curly leaped to their feet and dashed outside the tent, prepared, as they had planned. They peered anxiously toward the house on the bluff, and saw lights racing crazily about, upstairs and down.

"Well, you've got your wish!" Bing could not help reminding Giggles. "Something's sure happening!"

"And we're sure going to see what it is!" answered Giggles, starting forward, playing his flashlight over the ground.

Bing and Curly followed.

CHAPTER II

AN ASTOUNDING DISCOVERY

IT was slow traveling over the rough ground, making one's way around trees and clumps of bushes, clambering over jagged rocks which stuck their noses out of the scant soil covering the top of the bluff—slow traveling for boys unused to their surroundings. A minute seemed like half an hour now anyway, with the air reverberating the most terrifying cry.

"Ow . . . oooooh! Ow . . . oooooh!"

Giggles, Bing and Curly had cause to marvel at the speed with which Uncle Eb had apparently traversed this same distance between the spot where they had pitched camp and his house on the sheer edge of the bluff, especially since he had done it in the starkest kind of darkness. Several times Giggles, in the lead, had stubbed his toe and fallen even though his hand had held a flashlight which partially illumined the way.

"Be careful how you hold that rifle!" Bing had admonished Giggles once.

"It's all right, it's on safety," Giggles had answered. "Look out, here's a three-foot drop—then we're in the clearing!"

As the boys stumbled up the rise to the house the

weird noise suddenly ceased as though it had been choked off. They hesitated on the low steps leading up to the front door which was wide open. Perhaps it is not exactly correct to have described the door as "front" for it was the only entrance and exit to the house. The rear of the house, built almost flush with the face of the cliff, permitted of no doors unless one had wanted to step off into space and to have dropped the trifling distance of some three hundred feet, splash into the restless waters of Lake Michigan! No doors here, but a large, square window—unusually large—with a running seatlike beam inside it.

A sound now of scurrying feet, a something scraping over the floor, a groan.

"Douse your flashlights!" command Giggles, clicking his off.

Standing in the outer darkness the boys beheld a flaming torch, held head high, go flaring through the room nearest them and disappear toward the back.

"S-Say!" gasped Curly, in a muffled tone, "D-Did you see anybody with that light?"

"No . . ." said Bing, a prickly feeling running through his hair, "Gee, we're getting just about as goofy as Uncle Eb!"

"Tee, hee, hee!" giggled Giggles, "Isn't this *great?*"

From the basement of the house, sounding almost under the boys' feet, came a muffled cry for help . . . and the whimpering protest of a dog.

"There's old Spot—he's still on the job!" cried Curly.

"A brave dog, a very brave dog," recited Bing. Then to Giggles: "Hey, wait a minute! Where you going?"

"I'm going inside, of course! Where do you suppose?"

There was nothing else for Bing and Curly to do but to trail along behind. That's all they had been doing ever since they had known the impetuous Giggles. The fellow didn't seem to have the least sense of fear. He had always wanted to be right in the midst of things. Hadn't he spent hours hanging around the police and fire departments of Bean Blossom just hoping that, if some big catastrophe *had* to happen, it would happen while he was where he could be in on the opening scene? Oh, yes, Giggles had just doted on the misfortunes of others. He had stopped a runaway horse once and had gotten such a big kick out of it that, as he said, he had almost been tempted to scare other horses into running away so that he could experience the sensation of stopping them all over again. Nothing wrong in that desire, for Giggles would never have done such a thing. It only went to show what a red-blooded all-boy he really was. And Bing and Curly, while not quite so outwardly adventuresome, were not far behind him. Only about two feet—and those two feet their own!

"My flashlight's enough," directed Giggles as he

24

entered the large hallway. "Follow close, on tiptoes
. . . hello!"

The room opening immediately off of the hallway
was in the wildest disorder. A crude cot which
Uncle Eb had undoubtedly used to sleep upon, on
the rare occasions when he did sleep, had been turned
topsy-turvy. The thin mattress had been torn to
shreds and the stuffing scattered all over. The rip-
ping had evidently been done with an exceedingly
sharp knife. Other objects in the room had suffered violence also. A hole had been hacked in the
stone wall and a large rock dislodged. All this the
boys took in at a glance.

"Guess Uncle Eb was right," deduced Giggles, in
an undertone. "Somebody wants something he's
got. Wonder what it is?"

Now a peculiar, long-drawn-out creaking sound, as
of a heavy object being raised, the sound coming up
from below. Then a cry of triumph, the creaking
sound again, a sharp, slamming crack, and silence.

Giggles went ahead, beckoning with a hand which
clutched his rifle. The boys crept through another
room which was even more littered up than the first.
The next room brought them to the rear of the
house and the great window which looked out over
Lake Michigan. Of course there was nothing to
see out of it now but inky blackness, for the sky was
overcast. Giggles glanced down at the phos-
phorescent dial of his wrist watch.

Two o'clock!

"Funny . . . I don't see any way to the cellar," whispered Giggles, turning completely about.

"It doesn't look like the man who built this house intended any one to know there was a cellar, does it?" speculated Curly, after a minute spent in searching.

Bing felt along the stone wall, testily.

"Say, this house was sure well built. You'd never be able to push this off into the lake! Might look like it from outside but . . . whoa, here! What's this?"

A section of the apparently massive stone wall gave unexpectedly under Bing's pressure and swung silently away from him, leaving a widening gap. As it did so, disclosing a narrow landing and stairs leading down to the right, as one faced the opening, the three chums stared, amazed.

"Gee, that stone door must be perfectly balanced to do that!" exclaimed Giggles, thrilled. "Hats off to you, Bing. You're a real explorer!" Giggles went to step foot upon the landing.

"Not so fast!" commanded Bing, cautiously. "How'd that door go closed again after whoever it was opened it first?"

"Gee!" whispered Curly, excitedly. "How *did* it?"

"It's a cinch whoever opened it didn't stop to push it shut after him," reasoned Bing, "Look how the front door was left wide open . . . look at how the house was wrecked! The ones that entered this

house haven't tried to cover up their doings at all
. . . they've just run wild!"

"A—a door like that couldn't close itself . . ."
decided Giggles, eyeing it curiously.

"It couldn't, eh? Look at that!"

Bing grabbed Giggles' arm.

Sure enough—the stone partition had come to a
stop and had reversed its swinging motion, starting
back to again fill in the wall!

"Well—wouldn't that *get* you?"

"See, if we'd gone downstairs we'd have been
caught—sealed up, perhaps, in that cellar—just like
they were!" pointed out Bing, in a hoarse whisper.
"I'll bet you this door only opens from the outside!"

"Which means we've got to find some way to prop
it open," said Giggles, looking about.

Curly went into the next room, using his flashlight,
and came back with the leg of a table.

"Will this do?" he asked.

"We'll see," answered Bing, "We've got to wait
for this door to come clear shut first, before we can
open it again."

When the stone partition had settled smoothly
into place, the boys were forced to admire the workmanship which had so cleverly concealed the door's
presence. Once more Bing leaned against the wall
and once more the wall swung slowly out. It was
then that he discovered a hole in the door casing, a
barlike hole which obviously ran between the walls
into the room beyond. Giggles, going into this room

27

to investigate, returned with the information that the hole hacked in the wall had been for the purpose of reaching a rod and pulling it part way out.

"The rod, when in, pushed straight through a hole in the door and into the wall on the other side, locking the door tighter than tight," announced Bing, on examination. "I *thought* I discovered this door too easily. I never would have found it if some one else hadn't found the key and opened it before me! Say, this thing is getting mysterious!"

"*Getting* mysterious?" said Curly. "It's *got!*"

He inserted the table leg in the opening between the casing and the stone partition as the door reached its maximum swing. Breathlessly the three watched the heavy stone section pause and then shudder as it started back. Closing upon the table leg, the door gave a faint crunching protest, and was still.

"All right!" said Giggles, "Now we'll see what's doing below." He stepped down upon the stair landing and faced to the right. But, on turning, he beheld a sight which caused his eyes to bulge; the flashlight wavered in his hand; he whipped his rifle toward his shoulder.

"What's the matter?" demanded Bing and Curly, pushing forward, raising their hatchets.

Giggles stumbled back, making way so that his two chums could look in.

"Tee, hee, hee!" he giggled, nervously. "I'm not used to meeting fellows like him without an introduction!"

Hearts palpitating, Bing and Curly crowded down upon the landing and stood dumbfounded.

There before them, on the wall above the stairs, and in a grotesquely defiant attitude, hung a hideously posed skeleton! The body had been fastened to the wall much as a specimen in zoölogy is mounted on a strip of cardboard, the arms, legs and head having been secured with heavy rawhide bands so that the effect was one of a ghastly scarecrow, attired in a faded blue jacket and sailor breeches, the clothes tattered and slouched down over the loosely strung bones, a ghastly scarecrow with right arm rigidly extended, fist closed, the clenched brittle fingers seeming to speak a warning!

But, as startling as this sight was, the boys were more moved by an ominous piece of board which had been nailed above the skull and on which was carved the words:

WOE UNTO HIM WHO PASSES BENEATH MY BONES

E. B.

"E. B.?" repeated Giggles, thoughtfully, "E. B.? Why, gee whizz! That's old Ebenezer Beecher himself—Uncle Eb's grandfather!"

"No—it can't be!" declared Curly, unbelievingly. "He went away and never came back. I've always heard that. . . ."

"Yeah . . . he went away all right," agreed Bing, shuddering instinctively, "And maybe he came back dead, but he came back just the same, and we're

29

looking at all that's mortal of him right now! E. B.!
Say, what a sensation this would cause in old Bean
Blossom!"

"And to think—we've only just started!" reminded Giggles.

"Isn't that a *grand* thought!" reflected Bing.
"You know . . . I've a hunch that old Ebenezer
ordered this done! He knew that he couldn't live
forever and yet he wanted to go on protecting whatever he has to protect. It looks like he'd figured
that some day some one would break into this cellar
—some one who had feared him in real life—and
that, if they ran into his skeleton they'd lose their
nerve and turn around and back out!"

"Yes, but who'd do a thing like this, string old
Ebenezer up?" asked Curly, perplexed.

"Say, we haven't got time to figure anything out
now!" said Giggles, sharply. "It's up to us to see
what's become of poor Uncle Eb. He may have
been murdered!"

"That's so—I'd almost forgotten him!" exclaimed
Bing. "Wow . . . what a night. Sure we're not
dreaming?"

"If we are this is the swellest nightmare I've ever
had," declared Giggles. "Well, here goes!"

He pushed his way down the stairs, playing the
rays of the flashlight ahead of him.

"Woe unto you!" called Curly, in a low voice, re-
ferring to the words over the threatening skeleton.

"Ssssh!" warned Giggles, "Or it'll be woe unto all of us!"

Quietly—as quietly as was possible on the creaky stairs—the three chums felt their way down, down, what seemed an unusually long way down, to the floor of the cellar. There they became conscious of a damp chilliness and a musty smell, cavern-like walls which gave back leaping shadows, barren rooms, rough-hewn, stretching back toward what would have been the front of the house.

"Humph!" whispered Giggles finally. "Nothing down here that I can see. But there must be a secret room around some place, where they've taken Uncle Eb, a room where old E. B. probably hid something!"

"What would he hide?" demanded Curly, intensely practical.

"How do *I* know?" retorted Giggles, with a trace of disgust. "His false teeth, maybe. They were worth something in his day. . . ."

"Oh, shut up!" snapped Bing, impatiently. "This is serious!"

"Tee, hee, hee!" giggled Giggles. "Thanks for the information!"

Bing and Curly could not keep from grinning. Good old Giggles! Trust him to bolster up every one's nerve by making light of their situation. Trust him to get fun out of any happening. That was one mighty big reason why they were down in this cellar right now instead of several miles away—safe—and

31

still going! An adventure with Giggles was something of a lark thrown in. But it remained to be seen how much of a lark this was going to be.

Bing, standing near the wall of the furthermost room, distinctly felt something brush against his leg. He jumped.

"Hey!"

Almost simultaneously, Curly, near by, jumped also and hollered. Giggles, some feet away, turned quickly.

"Well?"

"My leg!" gasped Bing. "Something touched it!"

"Mine, too!" said Curly. "Both of 'em!"

Giggles came over, playing his flashlight about. He saw nothing; neither Bing nor Curly could see anything.

"You're crazy!" announced Giggles, quietly. "It's your nerves!"

"No, sir, it was something *alive!*" insisted Bing. "Something . . ."

"Yeow!" moaned Giggles, suddenly, making a wild leap. "I'll say it's something! Look out!"

The three prepared to give battle. Somewhere in the darkened confines of that musty room was a something that had boldly bumped into all of them— an invisible something! Flashlights could not succeed in catching it.

Finally a low, terrified whine. . . .

"Spot!" laughed Bing, relieved. "Ha! Ha! That's a good one on us!"

"Here, boy!" coaxed Giggles, stooping down and looking about. "Where are you?"

Uncle Eb's "very brave dog," now very much cowed, body quivering, dragged himself out of a shadowed corner, and advanced across the floor, belly fashion, begging for mercy.

"We're not going to hurt you, fellow!" reassured Giggles, reaching out to pet the shivering cur. "What's happened here anyway? Where's Uncle Eb?"

At mention of his master's name the dog's body bristled, the ears flung back, and the whine grew into a piteous bark.

"Go find him!"

For answer the animal jumped to its feet and ran around in an excited circle, nosing along the wall, occasionally rearing up on his hind legs to paw with the forefeet. The three chums looked at one another significantly and followed Spot with their flashlights. At length the dog came to a place on the wall which he sniffed excitedly. Bending close, the chums could perceive a faint line in the otherwise solid rock formation. Bing traced the line with his fingers, going up on tiptoe until he had described the shape of a door just wide enough to permit one person to pass through at a time. . . . Bing put his weight against it but the doorlike partition failed to give. He called for help. Curley and Giggles came to his aid. Under their combined pressure the heavy section of the wall began to tip back, not as the other door had done, but from the top down!

"Be careful!" warned Giggles, "there may be trouble on the other side!"

But only pitch black darkness greeted them. The door, resisting their efforts at opening, remained down only so long as it was held. Spot was the first one through, bounding out of sight. Bing crawled in cautiously, using his flashlight to guide him. Curly followed and Giggles came last. As soon as they had passed over the door and taken their weight from it, the partition started silently back into place.

"Catch it!" cried Curly, "or we're trapped!"

"Let it go," said Bing, "it works on some old spring or weight device . . . see? We can pull it open easy from this side."

"Boy, old Ebenezer or somebody must have spent a lot of time figuring these doors out!" remarked Giggles. "Say, who'd have thought there'd be such a big cellar under this house? We must be quite a ways under ground right now and. . . ."

"Bow-wow-wow! Wow-wow! Bow-wow-wow!"

"Darn that dog! We ought to 'ave left him behind."

"Grab him . . . choke that bark!"

The three chums groped their way across the cavernous room in the direction of Spot's noisy demonstration.

"Say, what do you know about this?" exclaimed Curly, spying out the cause of Spot's excitement.

34

"Another door—wide open this time—and in the floor! Gee! Here, fellows, quick! A cave . . . a CAVE!"

Bing and Giggles were at Curly's side in an instant, combining the power of their flashlights. Spot, rubbing up against their legs appealingly, knelt down and squirmed to the edge where he peered over, fearsomely. Looking in, the chums beheld crude stone steps leading down, a great yawning opening beyond. . . .

"Well, this beats anything I ever ran into!" said Giggles. "No hide nor hair of Uncle Eb—or anybody—just doors leading on and on."

"Ah!" said Bing, reaching down and picking up a wrinkled scrap of paper. "Here's something!"

Under the flashlight the paper proved to be a corner of a drawing, faded lines, a few meaningless figures.

"A map!" cried Curly. "A piece of a map!"

"Sure enough!" agreed Giggles, "that's what those somebodies were after; and they got it, too; and it looks like Uncle Eb had tried to get it away from them! Come on, you game?"

"Game for what?" asked Bing.

"To follow!"

"Huh!" answered Bing, scornfully. "You haven't stumped us yet. Get out the way, I'm going in first!"

"Tee, hee, hee!" giggled Giggles. "You've got another guess coming. There goes Spot!"

CHAPTER III

THE THREE FORKS

NO one in Bean Blossom would ever have imagined that there was such a thing as a cave within miles of the town and certainly no one would ever have suspected, if a cave *had* been known to exist, that the great bluff overlooking Lake Michigan on which Uncle Eb lived in his queer old house, contained a cave of uncharted dimensions!

If the discovery of the entrance to the cave had proven surprising to Giggles, Bing and Curly . . . then it is a doubly sure fact that the community round-about would have almost exploded with astonishment and wonder. Crafty old Ebenezer Beecher! He had either come upon this cave himself or learned about it from some early adventurer, making haste to hide it from view by having the house built over the cave's mouth. And the chances were that the cave's mouth had been camouflaged in the olden days by a growth of shrubbery, a mound of earth or some such barrier else other settlers, roaming the country, might have detected it. But this was mostly speculation and Giggles, Bing and Curly, as they felt their way down the stone steps to the floor of the cave, realized that there was no use trying to figure out how the cave happened to be there, or how it happened to be found, or why nobody seemed to have known anything about it. The cave just was—that was all. And here they were, venturing into it!

"Say, we want to be careful," warned Curly. "We're going right ahead here and not really thinking what we may be getting into. We don't know who's got Uncle Eb but it's a good bet that they're desperate characters. Uncle Eb's complained of terrible goings on for months and months. Now, who are *we* to be trooping down here, into this cave, after . . . after . . . ?"

"After what?" snapped Giggles.

"After trouble!" finished Curly.

The three chums stopped at the foot of the jagged stone steps and glanced about nervously, their eyes following the beams thrown by their flashlights as the beams focused upon a wide and irregular expanse of rock-ribbed walls. Nothing inviting and yet— nothing startling. Just cold, barren walls—and a narrow passageway at the other side of the cavernous room.

"Well, what you going to do—back out after we've gone this far?" asked Giggles.

"Of course he isn't," insisted Bing, his own courage slightly faltering. "He just doesn't want us to lose our heads over this thing, do you, Curly?"

"I don't want to lose *my* head anyway," answered Curly, making a clicking sound with his mouth and drawing a finger across his neck.

"Don't do that!" intreated Bing, glancing about. "Gee whizz, do you want to give a guy the creeps?"

Giggles snickered. "No danger of Curly losing his head . . . not when his brains are in his feet. You'd better watch out, Curly, or you'll be walking on your hands!"

"Oh, shut up! Let's see where that narrow path leads to. . . ."

"Better see where that fool dog Spot has gone to, first," suggested Giggles.

Bing and Curly swung off together, peering around the high ceilinged room. Giggles stepped cautiously toward the narrow opening in the wall which led out of the chamber into shadowy darkness.

"Giggles is a great kidder," said Curly, under his breath to Bing, "but don't you think I'm right about going easy. It was different before we knew there was a cave. But here we are away under ground and no telling . . ."

"Hey, what you doing—telling a bedtime story?" It was Giggles' voice, low and commanding. "There's nothing to really be scared of—yet. And we're the last ones in this cave, which means that we can be the first ones out. Come on, Curly. Quit growing white hairs before your time . . . I'm going in here after Spot!" And Giggles immediately disappeared.

Bing and Curly looked at one another consideringly. It had been one thing to call Giggles' dare and hurry down into the cave, but the spectacle of

38

it—the unbroken quiet of the place, the chilling damp of the air, the willowy shadows everywhere one turned, and the awesome size of the subterranean room which indicated the presence of other rooms, mysterious, perhaps, at least not exactly pleasant to contemplate—all these impressions had served as a sobering influence upon the two chums. And they hesitated.

"We could beat it out and hike to town and bring help back here in several hours," said Curly.

"Yes—and leave poor Uncle Eb to his fate," added Bing. "That's what's on Giggles' mind more than anything else. I *know* it. He's not doing this just for adventure. Not by a jug full. What if we were in Uncle Eb's place? Would we want the only ones who could help us running off to—?"

Bing never finished. His words froze on his lips. Curly shot out an arm and grasped Bing, tensely. In the distance, and seeming to come from the bowels of the cavern, sounded the same weird cry:

"Ow . . . ooooooh! Ow . . . ooooooooh!"

Then the excited barking of Spot, the dog, and the sharp crack of a rifle—Giggles' rifle!

Bing and Curly were inside the narrow passage in an instant, feeling their way along and calling out to Giggles that they were coming.

"We should never have let him go in here alone," censured Bing, anxiously. "We've got to stick together after this—all the way through!"

"Gee, there's just room for us to walk along, side by side!" commented Curly. "And say, isn't this the crookedest path you ever followed? Just like a corkscrew!"

"Ow . . . ooooooh!" came the cry, nearer this time.

"What's that sound like to you?" asked Bing. "Anything human?"

"I—I don't know," gasped Curly. "At any rate the thing that makes the noise is still alive, and if that's what Giggles shot at, he missed!"

Crack!

"There! He's shot again!" exclaimed Bing.

"And we're missing it all," regretted Curly, giving Bing a push. "Hurry up . . . let's get there!"

"Hey!" Bing stumbled and almost fell. "Hold on, what do you think I am—the volunteer fire department? We can't make any more speed than we are right now. Ah!"

Around a bend in the path, flashlights revealed a widening out, another turn, at right angles, but a room opening off this turn, and, in the door of the room, Spot, standing with the stub of his tail stiffly erect, looking within.

Bing and Curly hurried forward, brandishing their hatchets. They would have presented a funny spectacle at any other time but hatchets were the only weapons of defense they had, so it was natural for them to brandish them. Spot, on seeing Bing and Curly, let out a joyous bark. And then . . .

"Ow . . . oooooh! Ow . . . oooooh!"

That unearthly sound again—a sound of unusual penetration, a sound which seemed to add to the chill of the underground cavern, a sound which sent a chill into the marrow of human backbones.

"What *is* it?" demanded Bing, stopping in the doorway, Curly bringing up behind him.

"S-s-s-search me!" chattered Curly. "Look!"

There, not ten feet inside the room, lying prone on his stomach, was Giggles. His flashlight lay beside him, its rays pointing straight ahead. Giggles had his rifle clutched tight against the right shoulder. And the rifle was pointing at a white, vaporish form which illumined by the flashlight, seemed to tower and weave in silent but threatening fashion.

At sight of the apparition, Bing instinctively drew back his arm and hurled his hatchet with all the force he could muster. The form was quite a distance from him, at the extreme other side of this ragged-rocked room. But Bing's aim had been true.

Breathlessly, Bing and Curly followed the flight of the hurled hatchet—followed it until the hatchet struck its mark—struck it without making the slightest sound—and passed directly through it, and vanished from sight!

"Well, what do you know about that?"

Bing and Curly looked at one another in awe; and Giggles, straightening up, chanced a glance to his rear. He crawled to his feet slowly and, to the surprise of his two chums, turned his back upon the wavering form, retracing his steps to them.

"Tee, hee, hee!" snickered Giggles, as Spot bounded over and nosed around his shoe tops. "Some ghost, eh?"

"Ow . . . ooooooh!"

Only once this time, long drawn out . . . and sounding for all the world as though it came from that uncanny, sheetlike form which stood its ground, waving and writhing, raising its head sometimes to ten feet in height, then drooping as suddenly to less than five.

Giggles wheeled about at the sound, to stare perplexedly at the dancing, white image.

"It's that unearthly yell or scream or cry or moan or whatever-you-call-it that *gets* me," said Giggles.

"Well, *good night,* what about that . . . that ghost there?" asked Curly, keeping his flashlight centered upon it as much as a trembling hand would permit him.

Giggles turned to Bing with a low laugh.

"You're out a hatchet and I'm out two bullets," he said, "but the hatchet proved something. It proved to me that *that* ghost is nothing real. It's . . . it's . . . well, what do you say we go and see?"

"What?"

"G-g-ghosts aren't real anyway, are they?" asked Curly, cautiously.

"Excuse me," apologized Giggles. "My mistake.

42

This is not a real ghost, if that suits you any better. It's just like most other things. There's a perfectly natural explanation for them, if you can only find it. But this sure had me fooled for a few minutes!"

Giggles advanced into the spacious room directly toward the towering phantom. Spot kept pace with Giggles, eyeing the leaping form warily. Bing and Curly could do nothing but follow.

As the chums neared the peculiar shape their flash-lights brought it into bold relief. Through the transparent substance of the form was the narrowest slit in the wall . . . a jagged slit . . . dark and forbidding . . . but from this slit the form seemed to be oozing . . .

"Steam!" exclaimed Bing with all the enthusiasm of a discoverer.

"Vapor!" corrected Giggles. "And please don't get technical by asking me what causes it! But it's vapor just the same and it's coming right up through the floor of this cavern. . . . Boy, it gave me some scare when I first saw it!"

"Me, too," assented Curly. "Vapor, huh!"

"Ow . . . oooooooh! Ow . . . oooooooh!"

The three chums started violently. Spot cringed close to the ground, tail drooping.

"Th-that's not vapor!" declared Bing, emphatically.

"No, *that* isn't," admitted Giggles, listening intently. "But the sound comes through that same hole. It seems a good way off. You remember—

it's the same sound we heard above ground, when we were hiking it for Uncle Eb's house!"

"You bet it is," agreed Curly. "You only have to hear that sound once and you'll never forget it to your dying day. I've never heard a thing like it—not even any of the wild noises my radio set has made can touch it!"

"Must be a terrible sound," commented Bing, dryly.

Giggles completed an examination of the room. There were apparently no other entrances or exits save the one they had come through—and the slit in the wall, which led to—there was no way of determining where.

But Giggles did uncover something of peculiar interest. The rays of his flashlight came to rest on some white chalk marks emblazoned upon a smooth rock face. A shadowy figure and some crude lettering which said:

THE ROOM OF THE JUMPING LADY

"Tee, hee, hee!" giggled Giggles, when he read it. "Some ancient bird had a sense of humor!"

"And to think that you were so ungentlemanly as to shoot at her," reproved Bing, his fortitude returning.

"She's all right but her voice," agreed Curly. "But when she lets out that screech—*excuse* me!"

Giggles doffed his cap in mock politeness, making

44

a bow toward the vaporish form which never for one moment ceased in its rhythmic dancing—high and low, high and low.

"Sorry but we must be going," he said. "Thanks for your entertainment. You can keep Bing's hatchet as a souvenir. We can't get it back anyway as it's dropped down out of sight. Who knows, maybe we'll meet again. Bye, bye!"

Back once more in the passage, rounding the right-angled turn, Giggles stopped Bing and Curly for a conference.

"See here, fellows," he said, seriously. "It's pretty close to three A.M. We've monkeyed around down here and haven't managed to get very far. We haven't used very good system either. Now we'd better get right down to business and see to it that we don't make any boneheads from this minute on!"

"Well, Mr. General, I'm glad you've wakened up!" said Curly, vindictively. "I tried to get you to listen to reason when we first entered this cave. But no, you had to make some wise cracks about. . . ."

"You tried to get me to turn back!" snapped Giggles. "That's different. We don't turn back for anything!"

"Not even jumping ladies," sided in Bing, mischievously.

"All right, I'm willing to go *ahead,* but I'm mighty glad you've decided to keep your *head* about it," rejoined Curly, not to be outdone.

"There ought to be a law against puns the same as there is against using more than three syllable words," lamented Giggles. "Well, anyway, can either of you two fellows tell me why the Sam Hill we're all three of us using our flashlights at the same time?"

"Sure—to produce more light."

"Yeah . . . and burn up all our batteries at once so we'll be in darkness sooner," concluded Giggles. "We none of us know how long we're in this cave for, and I wouldn't relish groping around here, not being able to see where I was going or . . ."

Two flashlights snapped off simultaneously.

"All right, captain. It's your flashlight that burns out first, then. Lead the way!"

"Well, stick close to me. This path is narrow. Do what I do. If I drop down suddenly, you fellows drop in your tracks, too. I don't know about that dog. I wish in some ways he'd never have come along. Do you suppose we ought to drive him back?"

Spot seemed to know that Giggles was talking about him and began to whine, appealingly.

"Keep still then, if you want to come with us," ordered Giggles.

Spot's whine ceased but the tail began to wag.

"Wish I had four legs like Spot," remarked Curly, enviously, as the three chums started along the passageway again.

"Why?" asked Bing, before he thought.

46

"So if anything happened I could get away twice as fast," answered Curly.

"Shut up!" whispered Giggles in the lead. "You're worse than the dog!"

Gradually, as the boys followed the one and only visible passageway, it began to expand, the walls growing wider and wider apart, the ceiling rising in height. And now the chums were to view their first subterranean spectacle in the shape of rock formations for the ceiling over their heads became gnarled, the floor of the passageway which had been almost as smooth as a city street, grew rough with great blocks of rocks and the peculiar shadows that these irregularities cast one upon the other, presented a sight most unearthly—a sight which caused the chums to gasp time after time.

"Say—this is *some* cave!" breathed Curly. "There doesn't seem to be any end to it!"

Travel had been on a slow but steady downward path; there was no telling how many feet they were under the surface of the mammoth bluff. But one sure thing—the coldness was increasing.

"Do you know where you're going?" Bing finally called ahead to Giggles.

"No," the leader answered, "but I know I'm making a lot of detours to get there."

"I thought the center of the earth was a ball of fire," complained Curly. "I'm going to be disappointed if I find it's a cake of ice!"

Ten minutes later, Giggles' flashlight came upon a

gorgeous scene. He ordered the flashlights of his two chums brought into play here that they might explore a new and mysterious region. Stretching before them from the ceiling of the cave, now about two hundred feet high, were giant stalactites and beneath them, rearing up from the cavern's floor were huge, grotesquely shaped stalagmites . . . these deposits of limestone having been formed at some time in the dim, dead past by the drip, drip, dripping of water. It was a sight to cause one's blood to tingle strangely—the uncanny silence of it all, the marvelous beauty, the changing scenes as the illumination was shifted from one part of the yawning chasm to another.

"Why—there's three passageways ahead!" exclaimed Giggles, pointing them out with his flashlight. "See the one to the left under that queer, low arch, then the one not so far from it, almost right in front of where we're standing; the opening under that great, overhanging rock; and the third passageway directly on our right where the ceiling is so high?"

"We want to watch our step from now on," cautioned Curly, looking back of him apprehensively. "Gee, if we'd ever get lost down here!"

"It *is* getting kind of complicated," observed Bing. "Gives me an idea for a new kind of cross word puzzle!"

"Look at that big high cliff in front of us," directed Curly. "Doesn't it stick up in the air, though?

I'll bet it's made up of millions of jagged rocks. How would you like to try to climb it?"

Curly examined the steep, barrier-like formation which stood between the second and third passageways, from the left, in front of them. He went over the cliff with his flashlight, studying the unusual crevices.

"Bow-wow-wow-wow! Bow-wow-wow-wow! Wow-wow!"

Something had excited Spot. Body bristled, the little dog crouched on his haunches, head held high, eyes gleaming.

"What's he see?" asked Bing, curiously.

The barking sounded hollow and queer in this cavernous place, not much like a bark at all.

"He sees something up on that cliff!" said Curly, excitedly. "Follow his eyes with your flashlight, will you?"

Bing did. So did Giggles. And what they saw caused them to stare unbelievingly.

Standing on the top of a projecting rock, high up on the cliff and looking down at them, was the figure of a little man. A man such as the three chums had never seen before; a man who, despite his remarkable smallness of stature, struck fear in their hearts. For his face was wrinkled and old-looking, a particularly large head considering the size of the body, a body which could not have been more than three and a half feet in height!

"A—a dwarf man!" cried out Giggles.

"And he's got some pistols!" warned Bing. "Duck, quick!"

The boys dropped down just in time. Two shots rang out, bullets chipping pieces off of nearby rocks.

"Tee, hee, hee!" giggled Giggles, "the little rascal!" But Giggles' giggle was only on the surface. He was doing some fast thinking. "Keep your flashlights off," he commanded in an undertone. The three chums knelt, hearts pounding, in utter darkness. They waited anxiously while Giggles' wrist watch ticked off five minutes which seemed like five hours.

"Guess maybe I wasn't right about their being desperate characters," reminded Curly.

"I should say so," whispered Bing. "If the dwarf is that tough what would a full grown man be like?"

"What I want to know is how he got away up there?" asked Curly.

"Or why he took a pot shot at us," added Giggles. "We hadn't done anything to him—yet."

"Yes, but we didn't see him first," said Bing, "and there's no telling what you'd have done after the way you shot at that Jumping Lady!"

"I suppose I'll never hear the last of that," deplored Giggles. "Well, we can't stay here this way. You stay down the way you are, Bing. I'm going to get my rifle into position and give little Nemo some of his own medicine if he's still up there. Ready? All right . . . let's have the light!"

Bing hit the spot with the first flash, and there, still standing, pistols ready, was the pigmy man!

But as soon as the light struck him, and before Giggles could sight or pull the trigger, a pair of long, black arms reached out from behind the dwarf and jerked him bodily backwards off his elevation through a hole in the cliff!

CHAPTER IV

FLASHING DAGGERS

IT took several pulsating moments before any one of the three chums could offer a remark to the sensational incident they had just witnessed. As startling as had been the spectacle of the dwarf man staring down upon them, the vision of two, long, black, shiny arms stretching out to whisk the pygmy from the projecting rock had all but shocked Giggles, Bing, and Curly speechless.

Bing kept his flashlight playing upon the spot where the dwarf man had disappeared but nothing else happened. The great cavern was as still and cold as a tomb. Uncle Eb's very brave dog acted as though he would have been glad to have exchanged his breed for a shepherd dog with long, shaggy hair. Spot shivered and shook and whimpered. The three chums shivered too, but it wasn't so much from the cool dampness of the air as it was from the prickly chilliness of their spines.

"Did you see what I saw?" Giggles finally asked.

"Well, did *you* see what *I* saw?" Bing asked, in return.

"Black arms!" said Curly, recovering his voice. "Black arms as long as the dwarf was tall, sticking right out of black space, grabbing him up as though he was a feather!"

"Yep—guess my eyes are all right," decided Giggles.

"Mine, too," thrilled Bing. "I'm ready to believe anything Uncle Eb ever said now. Headless men, swords slashing through the air without any hands holding them, human yells coming from where no human beings are. Shucks! That stuff's going to be all pink tea before we get through here. I can feel it!"

"Well—control your feelings," urged Curly. "I'm having a few of my own!"

"What'll we do now?" asked Bing, uneasily.

"That's just what I was wondering," said Giggles. "This thing about has me stumped for the minute."

"Listen!" commanded Curly.

Far off, sounding as though the barrier of several walls and passages were between it, came the low, screaming cry of a human voice—a voice beseeching help. The shivering Spot, cocking his ears, strained forward that he might hear the better. Then he commenced an excited yowling.

"It's Uncle Eb!" exclaimed Giggles. "I'm positive of it. And he must know we're on his trail by the rumpus we've kicked up. Come on, fellows!"

"Where are you going?"

"To follow that sound while it lasts!"

The cry led them on the fork to the right with

Spot trotting eagerly in front. But the cry died out almost as they started, seeming more as though it was cut off than that it had actually stopped.

"They're on the move some place," deduced Bing. "And they're forcing Uncle Eb along with them!"

"Keep your voice down," warned Giggles. "Don't ever talk above a whisper!"

Feeling their way around rough depressions in the floor and climbing over small stalagmites which proved momentary bars to progress, the three chums finally came to an abrupt left turn, the main passageway running on straight ahead.

"Hello! Here's where things begin to get complicated," said Curly. "Isn't it about time we were marking the way we've come so we'll have some chance of finding our way back?"

"I was just thinking of that," replied Giggles, "I believe I could draw a pretty good map of as far as we've gone now, but . . ."

"But I'd hate to trust to any map you might draw to get us out of here if we got lost," finished Bing.

"So would I!" agreed Giggles. "All right. Curly, let's see how much of a dent your hatchet can make in that limestone wall. Cut out an 'X' if you can."

Curly picked out a place on the wall, shoulder high, and struck it a test blow. A shower of fragments flew about. The surface of the rock was so brittle that it could not withstand the slightest tap. But, successive blows left a jagged white scar in place of a somber gray which mark the boys decided

54

they could not mistake. Curly duplicated the mark on the inside of the left turn, which passageway the three chums elected to follow.

"Must be getting along toward morning, isn't it?" inquired Bing.

"Sure is," grunted Giggles. "But it doesn't look as though we're going to see the sun rise!"

"Hope we get out in time to see it set!" voiced Curly, fervently.

"Don't worry about that," assured Giggles. "If we don't find Uncle Eb by noon we'll—"

"Bow-wow! Bow-wow-wow!"

Spot had found something again. He was a most disturbing dog because, until the three chums were able to discover what Spot was barking about, they suffered agony. This time, however, Spot came running back with an object in his mouth which he held up joyously to Giggles.

The object was a shabby, pointed sailor's cap!

"Spot, you're some dog," congratulated Giggles. "We're on the right track, guys! Here's Uncle Eb's lid!"

"Let me have it," entreated Curly, who was bareheaded. He took the cap Giggles tossed him and put it on his head. The cap slid down almost over his eyes.

"Tee, hee, hee!" giggled Giggles. "Good thing your ears are so big!"

"Oh, shut up!" ordered Curly, "I'd rather have big ears than a big head!"

Spot kept up his excited barking.

"That dog has about as much sense as a solid mahogany dumbbell," said Bing, stooping down to slap Spot. "Keep quiet, will you?"

"There's no use talking, he's going to get us in dutch," declared Giggles. "We've got to tie him up some way and leave him here until we get back. This thing's getting too ticklish to risk having Spot ki-yi us into trouble."

"I've got some light rope—a short piece of it," informed Curly. "Piece I used to tie up my pack."

"Great, give it here!"

Bing caught Spot and dragged the wondering dog over to Giggles. Spot had no collar on and Giggles made a slip noose to fit about Spot's neck. Spot was fairly quiet until he discovered what was happening and then he put up a frantic struggle—scraping, snapping and pleading—all to no avail.

"Hate to do it, old fellow, but you're worse than a brass band on Sunday," said Giggles. "And we're due to face enough music as it is."

"What you going to tie him to?" asked Curly, looking about.

A thin but sturdy pillar of rock protruded from the floor of the passageway not far distant. Giggles led Spot to this and wound the rope about it several times after making sure that the pillar was stout enough to hold.

"Seems almost criminal to leave Spot, doesn't it?" said Bing, as the poor dog groveled and licked at Giggles' feet and exhausted every word and gesture in dog language which said, "Please, please, let me go with you!"

"Yeah—it's tough," admitted Giggles. "And I wouldn't do it if I didn't have more sympathy for ourselves than I do for Spot. Uncle Eb's second mate means all right, but he'd be as dangerous around us now as a stick of dynamite!"

The three chums pushed on, taking a last glimpse of Spot, tugging at his leash and whining piteously as they made a slight jog to the left out of sight, coming upon another break in the path. Curly, without waiting to be instructed, cut a niche in the wall producing a similar white scar.

"Not very healthy exercise for the hatchet," he said, ruefully.

Giggles decided to take the passageway to the left.

"Don't know why," he explained, "except I have a hunch it doubles back to a point about straight through from that first big room we were in."

There was a distinct mental tension to penetrating into the interior of this cave; following awesome passageways with their leering shadows; groping one's way around jagged blocks of stone; not knowing what moment one might come upon a strange sight or immediate danger!

Finally Giggles, in the lead, uttered a low cry. The path had blossomed out into another great room, much larger than the first and much more staggering to gaze upon. The room was divided into fragmentary partitions which might, at one time, have been other rooms, but which were now crumbled or fallen away. Stalactites hung from the ceiling like immense icicles and the stupendous cavern was studded on all sides with delicately tinted crystalline onyx marble which sparkled and shone under the rays of the flashlight. Picking their way about, Giggles, Bing and Curly moved forward until they came to a crude, winding stair which led up and up. This stair the three chums decided to climb, Giggles having another of his hunches. At the top, crawling upon a leveled off elevation which permitted a commanding view of the whole interior, Giggles stood upright and exclaimed.

"Just as I thought! Look here, see this hole— head high?" He stuck his flashlight through it and peered out. Bing and Curly staring over his shoulder.

The three chums saw a ledge, and beyond, many feet below, the big room where they had been when they had sighted the dwarf man!

"Gee!" said Curly, pushing Uncle Eb's cap back on his head, "we're standing right now where Mr. Runt was and . . . the black arms!"

"That's what we are!" said Giggles, giving a nervous glance about.

"What's that just above there?" asked Bing, pointing. "Some sort of picture on the rock, isn't it?"

58

Gazing at the point indicated, the boys saw a rather stiff drawing, in what appeared to be white chalk but which proved indelible under an attempt to rub off. The drawing represented the crow's nest, a box or perch near the top of a ship's mast, and a sailor in it, hand shading his eyes, staring out, presumably over the water. Under the drawing was the roughly scrolled words:

THE LOOKOUT

"Ideal place for a lookout, I'll say," grunted Giggles. "We're two hundred feet up from the floor of this cave . . . easy. And we can see through to the first big room from the back here. Begins to look like there was something doing in this cave in the old days, eh?"

Bing and Curly nodded. They were busy plying their flashlights about over the vast cavern beneath them, fearing they knew not exactly what, but fearing just the same!

"One thing," remarked Giggles as he started to descend the treacherous stair, "we know right where we are. There's some consolation in that."

"Ow . . . ooooooh!"

Giggles, Bing and Curly ducked instinctively. The sound was close at hand, the uncanny cry seeming to ring through the cavern.

"Slide down . . . out of sight," ordered Giggles, hoarsely. He took a firmer hold of his rifle.

It took some time to reach the floor of the cave, and reach it in comparative silence. The three chums could hear each other's labored breathing and it seemed to them as though their drawing of breaths could be heard from one end of the cave to the other. This was only their imagination, of course, but it didn't help their feelings any to have this distorted impression!

Once the foot of the stair was reached, Bing and Curly crept cautiously behind Giggles who kept his flashlight closely concealed, using it only to distinguish the step ahead. They came to a stone partition, wall-like, and worked their way around it, finding themselves at last in a three-sided room. The room was oblong, very long and narrow, the two side walls stretching out for some distance after the fashion of a great hall or corridor except that a wall joined the two side walls together at the other end. It was at the far end that the chums came upon a peculiar block of wood, square and heavy. The block had evidently been placed in position by human hands. Its surface was scarred by what appeared to be literally thousands of sharp depressions. And the block was spattered with dull red stains which had dried in the wood. A hollowed out portion in the middle was the most significant thing about it however, except for a few strips of leather attached to it.

"Wow! Do you *get* what this is?" Bing asked, a tight feeling coming across his temples.

"What?"

"Some kind of torture device. Watch!" Bing
turned his back to the wooden block and fitted his
body into the hollowed out portion; then he stretched
his arms out to the sides. The wrist of his left
arm touched a hanging strip of leather; the right
leg touched another, just above the knee. "See, they
strapped people up to this for some reason, and . . .
and stabbed them or . . . or something!"

"Get your knees out the way," directed Giggles,
stooping over. "There's some words carved in the
board." The wording was so worn and so hacked
up with stab marks that Giggles had to read it by
tracing it over with his fingers.

"The . . . the dagger board!" he announced,
tremulously. "Gee!"

"I wondered what all those nicks were from,"
said Curly. "Get away from there, Bing. I don't
like to see you imitating a living target!"

"Ha! Ha!" laughed Bing, enjoying the situation,
with the rays from Giggles' flashlight full upon him.
"Nothing to be scared of now. . . ."

Z-z-z-z-z-zing!

Something sung through the air, passing directly
between Giggles and Curly, striking the wood with
a dull spat. Giggles, horror-stricken, could only
gaze at the wooden block and Bing's terrified eyes
as his chum pulled at a black-handled object which
had pierced his blouse at the right shoulder and
buried itself in the wood. It was the kind of fas-

cination that a snake sometimes has for its human
victim which keeps the individual paralyzed for the
fraction of a second else Giggles would surely have
clicked off his flashlight or turned it away from the
board against which Bing was so perfectly sil-
houetted.

"Help!" cried Bing, "it's a *dagger!* Giggles . . .
the light!"

Z-z-z-z-z-z-zing!

A second dagger whistling through the air and
smack!—within two inches of Bing's head! Curly
grabbed frantically for Giggles' arm as Giggles came
to his senses and jerked the flashlight toward the
floor, smothering the light.

"Bing—all right?" he asked, anxiously, in the
darkness.

"Yes . . ." answered Bing, dropping down beside
his two chums. "Say, what a close call!"

And then, from the other end of the long room—
the only end at which there was any way of escape—
came that frightful reverberating sound!

"Ow . . . ooooooh!"

Instantly Giggles raised his flashlight and made
a sweeping pass with it. The searching beam caught
for a moment an imposing figure . . . a figure just
in the midst of another "Ow . . . oooooh!" Then
the figure, even as the light held it in view, dropped
suddenly and mysteriously out of sight.

"An Indian!" gasped Curly.

"All decked out, too, just like he was on the war path!" added Bing.

"Tee, hee, hee!" giggled Giggles. "I'm sure glad I know where that 'Ow-ooh' comes from anyway!"

"I don't know whether I'm glad or not," said Curly, uncertainly. "Good night . . . a dwarf man who shoots at us, big black arms, and a murderous-looking Indian who throws daggers as straight as bullets!"

"Don't worry about that," urged Bing. "That's all past tense now. Just do a little worrying about how we're going to get out of this place with a whole skin, will you?"

CHAPTER V

THE BLACK SHADOW

HEMMED in by three walls and menaced by the thoughts of the savagely attired Indian they had so shortly glimpsed at the open end of the room, the three chums crouched, uncertain what move to make next.

"Do you suppose Chief Ow-ooh's waiting for us?" whispered Giggles, after a long moment of creepy silence.

"Can't prove it by me," replied Bing, in an undertone. "He certainly disappeared quick when you flashed the light on him. Gee, I'm not crazy to have him fling any more daggers my way, I'll tell you that!"

"We've got to get out of here," decided Giggles, "Ow-ooh or no Ow-ooh." The nickname he had given the producer of this weird cry fitted so naturally that neither Bing nor Curly raised an objection to its use.

As Giggles crept carefully forward, his two chums followed, eyes straining into the darkness ahead, ears attuned to the slightest sound which might indicate the presence of some unknown enemy.

"I—I wonder what we're going to see next?" speculated Curly, just loud enough for Bing and

Giggles to hear. "If I ever get out of this cave I'll never . . ."

"S-s-s-ssh!" warned Giggles. "What was that?"

"I didn't hear anything. . . ."

The three chums paused to listen, tensely.

"What did it sound like?"

"I don't know exactly—maybe my imagination —seemed as though I heard a dull blow— there!"

Bun-n-n-n-ng!

Afar off, or deep down, a low, lingering rumble.

"Some one trying to pound in a door or batter something down," deduced Curly.

"Sounded almost heavy enough for a blast," suggested Bing.

But the strange detonation was not repeated.

Again the boys resumed their venturesome progress toward the opening in the wall which led once more to the great room in which they had been before. To the right of a towering stone pillar, Giggles' flashlight spotted a rusty-colored box with lid thrown back.

"A chest!"

"Funny, why didn't we see it when we came in?"

"We came in on the other side of that pillar, that's why."

"Say . . . look here! Daggers! Several hundred of 'em! Oh, boy!"

Excitedly Giggles fell on his knees before the heavy iron chest and groped about inside, pulling out a handful of beautifully shaped, dart-like daggers.

"Here's what old Ow-ooh was throwing at us!"

Each dagger, upon close scrutiny, was found to be fashioned alike, all hand-wrought, of the most perfect workmanship except where a few were scarred from use. Many of the blades were stained —and with what looked very much like blood. Giggles felt of the piercing points and shuddered. Bing did likewise.

"I'll bet these daggers have cut many a human form out on that board," surmised Curly, nodding his head toward the end of the room from which they had just come. "Think of it—facing death in that manner—with knives flying at you. . . ."

"I *did!*" reminded Bing. "Ugh!"

"No—Ow-ooh!" corrected Giggles, with a smile. "You mustn't get your Indian words mixed."

It was a temptation to the boys to load up with daggers but they finally decided to take three apiece. The daggers made excellent weapons, either held in the hand or as a hurling threat, though neither Giggles, Bing nor Curly would venture any claims as to their marksmanship when it came to letting the knives go.

"I'd like to be a good dagger thrower," said Giggles, slipping the daggers under his belt.

"That's fine," rejoined Bing, sarcastically. "I'll arrange for Ow-ooh to give you lessons as soon as we meet him!"

A depression in the floor of the cave at the opening in the end wall accounted for the mysteriously sudden disappearance of the Indian when he was seen to drop from sight. This depression the boys came upon and examined, it being decided that the redskin had dropped upon all fours and crawled away in the darkness beyond the rays of their flashlight. No trace of any one was discovered and the chums picked up courage. Apparently no direct attempt was being made to do them bodily harm. At least it seemed as though, had their capture been actually desired, it could easily have been effected when they had foolishly wandered into the three-walled room.

"Whoever's in this cave is just trying to terrorize us!" guessed Curly. "They don't want to have anything to do with us unless they are forced to."

"All right, Sherlock," scoffed Bing. "But wait till you have the close call that I did."

"Say, quit bragging about it, will you?"

"Ow . . . ooooooooooh!"

"Humph!" snorted Giggles, in disgust, "there goes the cave loon again. Doesn't sound half bad when you know what it is. But what's he make the noise for?"

"Maybe to keep himself company."

"No danger, that cry would scare a fellow a mile away from himself!"

"Well, he's doing it for some good reason," insisted Giggles. "He's not just holloing into space and he's not doing it for our benefit either, because he was yelling like that before he ever saw us, or we, him!"

"Excuse me for changing the subject," broke in Bing, "but—what time is it?"

Giggles consulted his wrist watch.

"Jingo! A quarter after five!"

"And I'm getting hungry," announced Curly. "Who's going to share my chocolate bar?"

"Have you got a chocolate bar?" asked Bing, eagerly.

"Sure, hip pocket. Only one, though."

"Give it to me!" commanded Giggles, holding out his hand.

"Hey, where do you get that way? Where do you come in on this? You'll be lucky to get so much as one bite."

"Quit your kidding and pass that bar over!"

Curly stared at Giggles, testily.

"Go on—you can't bluff me. I know you!" Curly drew back and started to peel off the wrapper winking at Bing. "Imagine the nerve of that guy—ordering me to give up."

Curly never finished. Giggles made a quick lunge forward, seized his chum's wrist, gave it a sudden twist which caused him to release his hold on the bar of chocolate, and, holding Curly back, slipped the bar into the pocket of his outing jacket.

"Nobody's going to eat that chocolate bar yet," he said, quietly. "This isn't *all* a joke. We don't

know how long we're going to be down here. And
we may be a lot hungrier before we get out."

Bing and Curly glanced at one another soberly.

"Gee, you talk like we were lost!" protested Bing.

Giggles shook his head.

"Not yet. But we might as well figure on it in
advance. Then if we *are* lost we'll not be quite so
bad off."

"Say, you're getting cheerful all of a sudden!"

"Tee, hee, hee!" giggled Giggles. "Glad you
think so."

"Help! Help!"

The cry was shocking in its unexpectedness but a
considerable distance away. Yet the boys could
recognize the voice and it served to spur them on
into action.

"Isn't that queer?" gasped Bing. "That yell
comes from back the way we came." He pointed
to the left.

"That's not the way we came," said Giggles.

"Sure it is!"

Giggles pointed to the right.

"We came in this way."

Curly looked in both directions, perplexedly.

"Don't tell me we could get turned around in this
big room!" he exclaimed, eyes widening.

Giggles chuckled softly.

"I'm not saying a thing," he answered, "except
that I got hold of that chocolate bar just in time."

"We're not lost?" gasped Bing.

"N-no, perhaps not," rejoined Giggles, "but, now that you're in this room and want to get out, did you ever see so many passageways you can take?"

The chums followed the gleam of the flashlight as it was moved about. They had not noticed it before, in their awesome admiration of the vast interior, but low-hanging, irregular arches seemed to lead out from the cavern in confusing fashion. Whether all of them did or not, or whether they just opened into little recesses or brought up against scraggly walls, only could be told by investigation.

"Help!"

There was a note of terror in the voice as it vibrated through the long, dark passages of the great underground cave, a note which indicated immediate peril, a note of frenzy and despair.

"Lost or not, I'm going to make one last try to reach Uncle Eb!" decided Giggles. "We've let ourselves get sidetracked several times now but I got the direction of that call exactly then. It came right through this passageway in front of us."

"All right, let's go!" said Bing, tingling with excitement.

Making as good time as was possible over the rough floor, the three chums entered the passageway and hurried along. Again Uncle Eb's voice quavered ahead of them, a trifle nearer this time, they imagined. The floor of the passage itself was fairly smooth and, using their three flashlights to speed up progress, Giggles, Bing and Curly had soon traversed a considerable distance, until the passage spread out into another room, smaller but no less beautiful in its oriental alabaster setting.

Not pausing to take note of this room as they had the other, the chums pressed forward, intent only on discovering what was happening to Uncle Eb. Their movement was arrested, however, by a sudden flare of fire emerging from the opposite side of a rock wall in the center of the room. The flame at once lighted up the interior in a ghastly manner, shadows leaping in perfect but leering harmony with the dancing flicker of the fire. Spellbound, Bing and Curly followed Giggles' example, falling prostrate upon the cave floor, extinguishing their flashlights. . . .

"A torch, just like we saw in the house!" whispered Curly, hoarsely.

"Yes, but . . . but . . . see *that!*" answered Giggles.

On the far wall, thrown in bold and terrifying relief, was the hideous shadow of a man . . . or man beast. The shadow was perhaps ten times normal size . . . showing a great ape-like head, massive shoulders, long, black arms!

"Those arms!" cried Bing, under his breath. "The arms that reached out and took the dwarf man . . . !"

"S-s-s-sh!" warned Giggles.

The shadow moved about, looking first one way,

then another, almost after the manner of a caged and restless gorilla. And the torch sputtered and flared and sputtered, waving backwards and forwards. The three chums, pressed against the floor, were grateful for the protecting darkness which a stone block cast over them. They did not care to be confronted with the owner of this monstrous shadow. It was easy to picture such a demon tearing them limb from limb.

"The torch!" spoke Curly, as the flaming light suddenly floated off across the room. "And nobody carrying it!"

The torch did appear to be traveling about without human aid. It was high up, too, so that the reflection from it caught the wall only halfway down and covered the yawning ceiling. All below was darkness, inky darkness. As the light moved, the horrifying black shadow moved with it. Once the shadow paused, raised its great arms over its head and stared straight toward the spot where the boys were hidden, fingers twitching. Giggles gripped his rifle; Bing laid hands on a dagger, and Curly grasped his hatchet firmly. How futile their little preparation to give battle actually was! They realized it even then, but what else could they do? The shadow man was big enough and brutal enough to destroy them with one, sweeping blow. But, to their intense relief, the shadow turned back and went groping along the wall as though in search of something.

72

"I—I—let's get out of here!" entreated Curly, "while we've got the chance!"

"You lie still!" commanded Giggles, clutching Curly's arm.

"Ow . . . oooooooh! Ow . . . oooooooh!" sounded the weird cry.

"*Help*. . . . HELP!" shrieked Uncle Eb's voice.

Bun-n-n-n-n-ng! The dull hammering blow again, all these sounds appearing close at hand as though they might be taking place in the next cavernous room beyond. The noises had an instant effect upon the torch which wavered and dipped.

"They've found it!" spoke a slight, squeaky voice.

"Umm . . . mebbe . . . mebbe not!" came a gruff, grunting answer.

Then the huge shadow vanished from the wall, simply sinking down out of sight. And the torch disappeared once more behind the rock barrier, leaving only a faint glow.

Giggles leaped to his feet, as quietly as possible. "Hurry! We've got to follow them!" he commanded, in a low tone.

"What! Follow that thing?"

"All right, stay behind if you want to. I'm going!"

And Giggles was gone.

"Gee, I'd like to see something that bird was really scared of," fretted Bing as he brought up the rear with Curly. But Curly did not answer. He was too busy keeping his teeth from chattering.

Rounding the rock wall, behind which the torch had plunged, the three chums came face to face with a sight which held them transfixed.

A brand of fire held high.

A tiny figure holding it.

The tiny figure perched upon the shoulder of the owner of the black shadow who towered at least seven feet in the air. . . . !

CHAPTER VI

A SHOCKING SIGHT

IF there is any truth in the assertion that one's hair stands on end when one is suddenly subjected to fright, Giggles, Bing and Curly must have felt their respective locks rise up and grow rigid. Curly started so violently that Uncle Eb's cap was jostled from his head and he only caught it by a wild one-handed stab. Bing and Giggles were conscious of their throats going dry and their Adam's apples refusing to budge.

The owner of the black shadow was a giant colored man, panther-like in his actions, garbed in a skin-tight black sweater, arms bare and glistening black, ragged khaki pants held in place by a knotted piece of rope! Seven leering feet of him, looking down upon the three chums with lips curled back in a hissing snarl, white teeth flashing, the dwarf man clinging to his neck with a small, white arm!

Perhaps the boys should have been used to unusual and pulsating sights by this time but somehow the experiences they had undergone had not served to make each new event any less thrilling. Giggles' first impulse was to bring his rifle into play, not as a means of doing violence, more as a threat.

"Ha! Ha! Ha!" boomed the colored giant as

he perceived Giggles' action. "You an' yo' pop gun!" His shadow and that of the dwarf's stood out behind them, ghostly, chilling.

The torch which the dwarf man held was fastened to the end of a stick, itself more than six feet long. Suddenly, and without the slightest warning, the dwarf man let this flaming torch fly—hurling it with all the force that his strength and the elevation could command. The torch, hurtling through the air at the end of the stick, became a fiery dart. Giggles, Bing and Curly saved themselves by dodging to one side, even then feeling the hot breath of the burning brand as it seared past. There was a flashing of bright embers as the torch struck a projecting stalagmite, shattering its light against the stone. And the cavern was plunged in darkness except for the lingering sparks and the faint glow of the dying torch itself.

"Quick! Your flashlights!" cried Giggles, making no pretense at keeping quiet now.

The flashlights clicked on together, sweeping the room. Under their concentrated glare, the chums beheld a fleeting glimpse of the huge black man, now a bent-over ape, feeling his way over the floor of the cavern toward a narrow passage, and on all fours, with the dwarf man riding on his back, tiny hands clutching the sweater at the neck! A fleeting glimpse of this and the peculiar pair were gone!

"Gee!" was all that Bing could say.

Curly could not find voice to say even that.

Giggles wheeled quickly and sought out the smoldering torch. He picked it up, tearing the torch itself from the long stick to which it was lashed.

"That stick explains why it looked like there was no one holding the torch," said Giggles, excitedly. "The dwarf carried it so high above his head . . . Ah! . . . I was wondering . . ."

Giggles peered at what was left of the torch, rubbing some of the charred portion away. Bing and Curly looked on, curiously, keeping wary eyes also on their surroundings.

"Why pay any attention to that old torch now?" demanded Bing, nervously, "no telling what may happen to us any minute. I'm for . . . !"

"Tee, hee, hee!" giggled Giggles. "Part of the mystery's solved anyway!"

"What?" asked Curly, impatiently.

"The mystery of where such a strange combination as an Indian, a dwarf and a giant black man came from," answered Giggles. "Or don't you care to know that?"

"Sure!"

"But you can't . . ."

"Easy! See what was printed on this torch. Part of it's burned off now . . . but there's enough left to tell."

Bing and Curly gazed intently at the fire brand which Giggles held up for their inspection. It was a manufactured product, the outer surface of the torch being a dull red in color . . . and some badly

77

smudged lettering which, carefully scrutinized, revealed a half-charred title.

. . . . EATEST SHOWS

"Well, I'll be dogged!" exclaimed Curly, surprised.

"Brockton's World's Greatest Shows!" filled in Bing. "Now wouldn't that stun you? But what are these birds doing off the road? Why aren't they with the circus? And what are they doing here? Why are they after Uncle Eb?"

"Wait a minute! Wait—a—minute!" cut in Giggles. "I just said I'd solved *part* of the mystery. Don't you think it would be a good idea to use your beans a little bit, too?"

Bing and Curly exchanged slightly sheepish glances.

"No . . . we're saving ours just like we are the flashlights, so our beans won't all wear out together," was Curly's comeback.

"Oh, I see," grinned Giggles. "Well, just so I know that I can count on your beans when they're needed. . . ."

"Yes, sir," promised Bing, jovially. "Mine's a brand new one—never been used."

Giggles' grin broke into a low laugh. "I can almost believe that," he said.

"All joshing aside," spoke up Curly, "it's sure a relief to have this much figured out. The sight of

78

that colored man just about drove me goofy. Now I'm prepared to see anything from an armless wonder to a calf with three tails!"

Giggles flashed his light in the direction in which the dwarf and the giant had gone.

"Well, supposing we follow the circus instead of talking about it," he suggested. "I haven't heard a peep out of Uncle Eb in the last ten minutes."

"Poor Uncle Eb!" sympathized Bing.

"Poor Spot!" sympathized Curly.

"That's right. Wonder how Spot *is* getting along, tied up in that passageway?" asked Bing.

"*Which* passageway?" emphasized Giggles.

"Gee, I never thought of that! Which?"

"Never mind. Spot's probably starved to death long ago," said Curly, gravely, putting a hand tenderly over his stomach region.

"Humph!" snorted Giggles. "That's a poor way to get your chocolate bar."

"Who said anything about a chocolate bar?" demanded Curly, with perfectly affected innocence.

Giggles gave Curly a reprimanding look as the three chums reached the passageway through which the human gorilla and his pygmy attendant had gone.

Passageways were passageways in this most astounding underground cave. It was extremely difficult to distinguish one from another unless it might be by the length or breadth or some identifying mark such as a peculiar stone formation.

"No chance of blazing a trail down here," Giggles decided. "Not with our equipment anyhow. If we'd had a big ball of twine we could have laid out a route beautifully. But we've gone so far now that we've just got to trust to luck, and whatever judgment we have."

Curly gazed sorrowfully at his hatchet. The blade was nicked in several places where it had made contact with stone.

"Sorry, old boy," he said, "your sacrifice was in vain."

"Cheer up," reassured Giggles, "that hatchet may be of real service any time."

"Hope so," rejoined Curly, running his finger along the edge of the blade. "It's complaining of having a *dull* time."

"Hey!" protested Bing, "pull another one like that and we'll be using friend hatchet on you!"

Curly obediently lapsed into silence. The three chums, Giggles as usual in the lead, started along the passageway. The path, at this point, was unbroken for some distance and veering slightly toward the right. Sometimes the chums were required to bend low to crawl under mammoth stalactites which pointed down from the ceiling like great frozen slabs.

"Wow . . . I hope this baby doesn't take a notion to drop off on me!" Giggles said once as he squirmed through a particularly tight place and glanced up at the great weight which hung above him.

"What I don't see is how big boy and little Nemo ever made it through here in the dark," said Bing. "I'd hate to attempt it."

"Probably *was* quite a trick," admitted Giggles. "But they'd probably been over the ground before and knew about what to expect."

"Even then . . ." started Curly, and stopped as a voice sounded close at hand.

"Come on, now! Don't give us none of that stuff! You're goin' to tell us what you know, and you're goin' to tell us quick. It's time we was gettin' out of this cave now. Been fiddlin' around here with you more'n three hours. Do you think we was born yesterday? Of course you kin read that map, and you know where that treasure's hid, too!"

"*Treasure!*" breathed Bing and Curly, pinching each other. "*Treasure?*"

"Shut up!" begged Giggles, "listen!"

The voice was coming from a room just a jog further on along the passageway. It was answered by the worn, pleading voice of Uncle Eb.

"Honest . . . honest to God, Mister, as honest as I never seen you before. I don't know nothin' about this here map, nor no treasure if there be any. My grandfather was crazy, I tell you . . . crazy . . . but a right powerful man . . . right powerful. I feared him, I did! And you'll be a fearin' him, too, if you don't let me go. Help! HELP!"

"Holler yer head off!" invited the big blustering

81

voice . . . a voice which the three chums could not recognize. "There's nobody within ten miles of you but them three little schoolboys . . . and I'm goin' to spank their wrists pretty soon and send 'em home to their mammas."

"Huh!" sniffed Giggles, pushing around the bend in the passage, Bing and Curly at his heels.

"Umm . . . better not do that," counseled another voice. "Better catch boys . . . no let go . . . no see mammas any more . . . no bother us then . . . any time . . . any place. . . ."

There came the sound of a hand slapping some one heartily on the back.

"Good idee, Redwood, good idee! You're a darn smart Indian. I'll leave the whole business to you."

"Ummmm!" was the satisfied response.

"Here, George, bring that fire over here!" ordered the big voice.

"No!" screamed Uncle Eb, "NO! I'll tell you . . . I'll tell . . . !"

Crouching in the passageway, the chums felt their hearts skip beats as they looked toward a narrow slit opening into the room where Uncle Eb was facing his terrible ordeal.

"Good night!" whispered Curly, in horror, "were they really going to brand him?"

"Sounded like it," nodded Giggles. "Or else put up a grand bluff at doing it. Wish I could get a look in that room. We've got to get Uncle Eb away from those fiends somehow. They're bad ones, all right, lots worse than I thought!"

"Yeah, we want to watch out for ourselves," warned Bing. "That Indian! He'd just as soon put a dagger through your heart as breathe. We don't want to run a chance of getting caught. . . . !"

"Little schoolboys!" scoffed Giggles. "The guy with the heavy voice called us 'little school boys.' Well, all I want is a chance to *show* him. Come on, fellows. Let's take a peek!"

It was a mad venture. Giggles knew it, and Bing knew it, and Curly knew it. But their presence in the vicinity had been made light of, and they had a certain amount of pride to go with their courage. And then, Uncle Eb was truly in very great danger. They would have been yellow pikers to have beaten a retreat now without at least seeing what they could do to liberate him.

"Well, we're waitin' fer you to tell us!" The big voice again.

The three chums crowded into the narrow slit, noiselessly, and worked their way to a point where they could gaze into the room. The sight which met their eyes was the most shocking of any they had witnessed heretofore, much more shocking. It was a sight to make blood feel as if it were freezing in one's veins, and then thawing out again under intense heat, and then freezing again. . . .

Standing over Uncle Eb, with a large hand placed upon his throat, was a big, strapping white man, the upper half of his body clothed in a dirty blue shirt, torn to ribbons, through which the huge muscles of the arms bulged, his broad back being turned toward the boys and feet set well apart. At the side of Uncle Eb crouched the seven-foot form of the colored giant with the bright red end of an iron rod pointed downward—a rod which had been heated in a fire, now a bank of coals in a far corner of the room. On the other side stood the Indian, holding a blazing torch aloft . . . the torch sending forth a wavering light which added to the gruesomeness of the sight. And beneath this torch, wrinkled face screwed up, sat the dwarf, a sheet of parchment paper with a torn-off corner smoothed out against his knees, which the boys instantly recognized as the map.

"Thought you said you was goin' to tell us!" insisted the white man, who appeared to be the ringleader.

Uncle Eb raised gnarled hands to his face and pulled feverishly at his beard. The whites of his eyes gleamed in terror.

"I don't know . . . I told you I didn't know . . . I can't tell anythin' I don't know . . . but don't brand me! Don't brand me!"

The white man released his hold upon Uncle Eb's throat and stepped back, hands on hips, to study the pitiful old fellow, consideringly.

"His gran'father . . . he not show my gran'father no mercy!" reminded the Indian addressed

84

as Redwood. "Him gonna tell. Him gonna tell lots o' things! You make him, or *I* make him!"

"See here, Uncle," persisted the white man. "First you say you're goin' to tell us, then you say you can't, you don't know. We been mighty decent with you up to now."

"Don't brand me!" begged the descendent of old Ebenezer Beecher. "Don't brand me!"

Uncle Eb crawled toward the white chieftain on his knees, imploringly, and, as he did so, the chums —watching breathlessly—heard the clink! clank! of a chain.

"Why, they've got him chained fast to the wall!" whispered Giggles. "See that iron clasp around his leg!"

As the boys looked on askance, the colored giant brought the smoking hot point of the iron rod within an inch of the victim's face. Uttering a loud, frenzied cry, Uncle Eb pitched forward upon the floor.

"Stop! Hands up, every one of you!"

Giggles unable to witness more, had sprung into action. Rifle pointed at the four surprised characters, he intended to browbeat them into releasing Uncle Eb if he could. Bing and Curly stood just behind, determined, and ready to back Giggles up in any step he might take.

The colored giant raised up to stare curiously at the slit-like entrance to the room; the Indian held his torch a bit higher to get a better view; the dwarf man scrambled to his feet, clutching the map to him; while the powerful white man turned slowly about in his tracks to reveal a domineering face, overbalanced by a vicious, protruding jaw.

"Ha! Ha! Ha!" laughed the black man. "De boy wid de pop gun!"

Crack!

A bullet sung off the iron rod and the white teeth of the black man disappeared behind startled lips.

"Tee, hee, hee!" giggled Giggles. "I can laugh, too! Pop gun, eh? I'll show you! Take the chains off that man there. Make it snappy!"

The colored giant consulted the white leader soberly. The white man nodded, hands twitching, chest heaving. He was roaring mad inside at being held at bay by a mere school boy. Had he only known, Giggles had flashed his most dangerous hand. He would not have shot to wound any one. He could not have brought himself to do that. Giggles had undertaken a big gamble which just now gave promise of winning.

There was a convulsive shudder from Uncle Eb. The grizzled face raised from the cave floor and stared out toward the narrow doorway. When he saw Giggles standing there, Uncle Eb's expression changed from one of terror to one of extreme joy. He reached out his arms and tried to lunge forward only to be tripped up by the chain.

"Boys!" he cried.

86

"Let him loose!" ordered Giggles, keeping his rifle trained.

The colored giant knelt down and fumbled with the chain.

"Get that map from the dwarf!" Bing whispered nervously in Giggles' ear.

"Bring me what you've got in your hands, *you!*" commanded Giggles, motioning at the pygmy man.

The dwarf looked up in alarm and glanced questioningly at the white chieftain who glowered at the boys with the ferocity of a maddened animal.

"Come on, get a wiggle on!" snapped Giggles. "Next time I shoot, I shoot to . . . !"

The dwarf man wiggled.

Keeping an eye on the dwarf as he shuffled lightly across the cave floor toward him, holding out the piece of parchment, Giggles also watched the progress of the colored giant in unfastening the chain from about Uncle Eb's legs.

"Here, Bing, you take that map," Giggles directed in an undertone.

Bing held out his hand, warily. As he did so, the chums were startled by a cry from Uncle Eb.

"He's not tryin' to unfasten me, boys, he's not tryin'!"

Then things happened.

The Indian, who had been standing as quietly and unmoving as a wooden image in front of a cigar store, suddenly dashed the torch he had been holding against the nearby wall. The room went instantly dark. Almost before Giggles could realize what had taken place, he felt a blow and the rifle struck from his grasp. Bing, who had been in the act of taking the map from the dwarf, had only the sensation of touching the parchment with his fingers when a sweeping rush of air seemed to whisk it out of his reach, and the thud of a small body striking the floor some distance away told, as plainly as though he could have seen, that the pygmy had been tossed violently to one side. Curly, nearest the outside passageway, grasped Bing by the shoulders and yanked him backwards. Bing, in turn, caught Giggles' arm.

"Quick!" urged Curly. "This way . . . follow my flashlight!"

The fact that the opening to the room was narrow, permitting only one person entrance or exit at a time, perhaps was the biggest factor in aiding the chums to reach the outside passageway ahead of their pursuers.

"Don't leave me, boys! Don't leave me!" wailed Uncle Eb after them.

But Giggles, Bing and Curly were in full retreat now, plunging to the right down the cavernous passage, conscious of the panting breath of some one behind them.

"Ow . . . oooooh!"

The Indian . . . using his murderous yell as a bloodhound on the trail of a human keeps up a continuous baying, for the purpose of keeping other pursuers informed as to the direction of the pursuit!

And behind the Indian, the savage bellowing of the white chieftain.

"Catch 'em! Don't let 'em get away! Oh, what I'll do to them rowdies when I get my mitts on 'em!"

"Tee, hee, hee!" giggled Giggles, as the three chums gained ground in the chase. "At least we've graduated from 'little school boys.' So, we're *rowdies* now? How nice!"

"Just so we're not goners!" gasped Bing. "Wow, that was a close call!"

"Was?" protested Curly glancing anxiously behind him, "Still is!"

CHAPTER VII

THE CAVE OF HORRORS

FOR the next ten minutes the three chums were too strenuously engaged in putting distance between them and their enemies to make further comment. A sharp, almost right angled turn in the passageway brought to their nostrils an unusually damp and musty smell, and the glimmering rays of Curly's flashlight revealed moisture standing out in places. The odor was anything but pleasant —an odor new to the boys, and one which made them hesitate to penetrate beyond a cavernous opening looming up ahead.

"Gee, what do you s'pose we're coming to?" asked Giggles, sniffing the air, anxiously.

"Got me!" answered Bing. "But I don't like it, whatever it is."

"Perhaps we'd better stop right here," suggested Curly, wavering, peering back into the darkness. "I don't hear any one after us now."

"Ow . . . oooooooh!"

"You don't?" retorted Giggles, swinging into motion. "I do! What's a little smell compared to that Indian? Come on!"

Bing and Curly needed no second bidding. They plunged through the cavernous opening and into a vast room which made the ray from the one flashlight look like the feeble flicker of a match. The atmosphere in this room was moist and heavy . . . the odor almost overwhelming in its mustiness. The three chums put hands to their noses as they staggered on, feet slipping in a peculiar slime—soft, clammy-like, earthen substance. Ghastly columns of fantastically shaped rocks hung from the lofty ceiling, projected from the walls or reared, in ungainly fashion, from the floor. These columns were plastered with the same uncanny residue which the boys had encountered underfoot.

"Gee, this is the queerest mess I ever got in!" exclaimed Curly, repulsively.

"Terrible!" emphasized Giggles, trying to extricate his feet from the gummy surface.

An instant later the three chums were startled by a strange whirring sound, dull at first, but growing in volume. The whirring soon became a rustling sort of roar. Bing and Giggles added the force of their flashlights to the one held by Curly and swept the yawning spaces of the cavern, fearsomely.

"Bats!" exclaimed Giggles, forcibly, "thousands of 'em!"

He had hardly made the outcry before the swirling cloud of winged creatures was upon them, fluttering dizzily toward their lights as June bugs flick about street arcs.

"Let's get out of here, quick!" entreated Bing, backing up and covering his face with his hands.

Bats . . . bats . . . everywhere! The cavern alive with them, scraping, clawing, crawling, creeping, *squeaking* BATS! Scores of them colliding with Giggles, Bing and Curly, clinging momentarily, catching in their clothes, brushing against their faces, whistling past and round and round! Ugh—what a loathsome sensation! The three chums beat the flying forms off with their hands and arms . . . using the short metal stubs of their flashlights. Curly even waved the hatchet but he was forced to abandon this as Giggles ordered lights out to see if total darkness would improve the situation, and Curly was too afraid of striking one of his pals.

"But, gee, how're we going to see our way out of here?" asked Bing, anxiously.

"Don't look like we are, if this keeps up!" answered Giggles, crouching down. "Don't try to fight 'em. Leave 'em alone and see if they'll let up!"

The bats were not really attacking them. They had just swirled into the cavern in such great numbers that a small portion of them had come in contact with the three chums, a contact which apparently was not any more enjoyed by the bats than by the humans! But it was quite probable, however, that the experience was proving far more terrifying to the latter.

Outside the cavern, in the narrow passageway through which the boys had come, the Indian, Redwood, halted, and listened. His features spread into a satisfied smile as he turned to address the burly white chieftain and the colored giant who stood behind.

"Ummm. Boys no trouble now. Bats show boys good time. Too good time. Redwood not go in there for million dollar. Two million dollar!"

"You're sure they went in there?" The white chieftain wished to make certain.

"Ummm. Tracks!" Redwood pointed to the soft, moist underfooting around the mouth of the forbidding interior. The colored giant raised another torch as high as the overhanging stalactite would permit.

"Good!" grunted the white chieftain, turning back, "where's Tiny Thumb and that map? I don't think he knows nothin' about readin' maps anyhow. And that sailor fellow's so nutty you can't get nothin' from him. I see right now it's up to me to find this here treasure . . . up to me!"

"My gran'father . . . he buried near treasure," volunteered Redwood. "He know too much about it. Find where he buried . . . find treasure!"

The Indian and the white chieftain and the colored giant retraced their footsteps down the passageway.

Giggles, Bing and Curly, struggling nearby, would have given much could they have overheard what was said. Now, in their efforts to escape the bats, they had wandered further away from the entrance, following down along a slimy wall, keeping their feet with difficulty, flashing on a light only long enough to glimpse the next step or two ahead, being constantly plagued by fuzzy, living things which seemed as thick as gnats only infinitely more torturous because of their comparatively huge size!

"I don't believe we're going in the right direction!" gasped Curly, finally.

"I *know* we're not," answered Giggles. "But just so we're going some place, any place, away from here!"

"That's just it!" objected Bing. "Maybe we're getting in deeper. Maybe there isn't any way out but the way we came in!"

"There must be!" insisted Giggles. "Those bats had to come from somewhere. They've been out all night. See—some of them are beginning to settle already. Inside an hour they'll all be asleep."

"Thank heaven for that!" breathed Curly, still guarding himself.

The whirring sound commenced to diminish in volume. And all the crags and pillars and walls of the great cavern began to be dotted with hanging bodies.

"I'll bet there's a passageway leading out to Lake Michigan through here!" reasoned Giggles. "These bats feed on insects . . . they've got to get out to get them. Can you imagine how many insects all these bats would have to have in a night? Wow!"

Bing and Curly shuddered. The fluttering creatures were so repulsive to them, so alarmingly close in their flutterings, that the touch of their furry forms made human flesh prickle.

"Gee, I thought it was bad enough when *one* bat got in my bedroom at home," said Bing. "What a wild time I had chasing him around till I opened the window and drove him out."

"Well, you won't drive these bats out," interposed Giggles. "We're in *their* home now, and they're driving *us* out!"

"No they're not," objected Curly. "We're going out of our own free will!"

Presently the mad flying about quieted down except for some few hundreds of the bats which seemed to be having more than ordinary difficulty in finding suitable roosting places. The chums, not so molested, paused in their groping flight, to gaze upon a scene not often given to man.

So thickly populated with bat life was the odorous cavern that it now appeared to have been constructed of the hideous-looking mammals, hanging upside down as they were to every possible crevice, one body seeming to cover another, a sleek, seething mass.

"Say—maybe Professor Larkin wouldn't give a lot to see this sight!" exclaimed Giggles. "He'd be for bringing his zoölogy class right down here to study the bats at first hand."

"Yes, he would!" kidded Curly. "If he ever saw a real live specimen of a bat, he'd throw up teaching. Remember the day I brought the water snake to school?"

"Never mind that story now," interrupted Giggles. "Does that look like a way out to you?"

He pointed with his flashlight toward a jagged ascent of rocks some distance ahead which seemed to lead up to a small opening. In front of them and behind, the cavernous interior stretched on and on for all they knew. They had made no attempt to do more than follow along the outside edge of it after their first, frenzied leap into the creeping habitat of the bats.

"We can soon find out what it is," rejoined Curly, with new optimism. "Let's take a look!"

Watching their footing, the three chums crept carefully over the slippery rocks and mounted the sloping rise to the opening Giggles had spotted.

"She sure goes somewhere!" announced Giggles, after peering in. "Just room for us to crawl through. Shall we chance it?"

"Why not?" asked Bing. "It wouldn't be the first thing we've chanced since entering this cave!"

"Have you still got that chocolate bar?" inquired Curly, of Giggles.

Giggles felt of his pocket.

"Yes," he answered, perfunctorily.

"I'm glad of that," replied Curly, with obvious relief.

"I wish you wouldn't keep reminding me of that chocolate bar," Giggles added, after a moment.

"Why not?"

"Because I'm getting hungry *myself* now!"

"Serves you right!" was Curly's retort.

Giggles was the first one through the aperture. He explored the surroundings as thoroughly as he could before beckoning to Bing and Curly to follow.

"At least it's dry in here," he informed.

"My, it seems like we're miles away from where we saw Uncle Eb, doesn't it?" said Bing, joining Giggles. "Here's hoping we never have to go back through where those bats are again!"

"I don't think we will," reassured Giggles. "This cave appears to be a perfect network of passageways, crossing and criss-crossing each other. You can't tell, we may be almost back to where we started from."

"Yes, and we may not be, too," presumed Curly, staring about. "It doesn't seem to bother you guys much, but I don't like this idea of being down here below ground, lost, and with only one chocolate bar between us and . . . !"

Giggles glanced at his wrist watch.

"Will *you* dry up? It's only six-thirty. Nobody takes a nibble until eight A.M. . . . and that's final!"

The small room that the chums found themselves in now possessed a high and peculiarly formed ceiling. The room itself tapered into another passageway which was of the winding kind. It was while pressing forward along this passageway that Bing suddenly cried out and pointed to a mark, shoulder high, on the wall. The mark was a white arrow with tip stained blood red, the arrow pointing straight ahead. Underneath the arrow was a characteristic wording, in white letters, easily readable despite their irregularity, with the flashlights played upon it.

IF YOU HAVE COME THIS FAR YOU ARE ON THE
RIGHT TRACK——FOLLOW YOUR NOSE!

E. B.

"Hot stuff!" cried Curly, all excited. "We're on the trail of the treasure sure. Good thing we were forced into the cave with the bats!"

Giggles stood studying the sign before making comment.

"Hmmm!" he remarked, finally. "Old Ebenezer Beecher must have felt pretty certain that nobody would ever come this far. Either that or he's done a piece of grand kidding, leading any one who'd take the trouble to look for his treasure on a wild goose chase."

"Wild is right!" agreed Bing.

"Wish we'd gotten hold of the map."

"Who doesn't?"

"I've still got that corner of it," reminded Bing. "And I *touched* the rest of it . . . don't forget that!"

"Let's see the corner again," commanded Giggles.

"There were some figures on it . . . . and it may just be possible."

Bing produced the torn off corner of parchment paper and smoothed it out so that Giggles could examine it. Curly looked over Giggles' shoulder.

"Wow! Wow! WOW!" yelled Giggles suddenly, dancing a jig. "I've got it, guys. I've got it! No wonder that gang can't figure out how to locate the treasure. We've got the KEY!"

"*We* have?"

"How do you make that out?"

"Look!"

With his finger Giggles traced the lines of a drawing, faded, but made clearer by such tracing.

"See what that is?"

"Why . . . why it looks like a . . . a part of a face, an eye, and . . . and . . . a nose!" determined Bing.

"That's right—a NOSE!" fairly shouted Giggles, pointing up to the sign on the wall. *"Follow your nose. . . . That's the key!"*

Bing and Curly stared at each other, nerves tingling.

"By thunder!" Curly ejaculated.

"Giggles, you're a wonder!" complimented Bing.

"Tee, hee, hee!" giggled Giggles. "Take you all this time to find it out?"

Curly grabbed Giggles' arm.

"Come on, let's hurry up and follow our noses. We may be almost on top of the treasure now!"

But Giggles' first move was to get the precious piece of map from Bing.

"I'm going to carry that from now on, if you don't mind," he said. "What wouldn't the big white chieftain give for it if he knew . . . eh?"

"His nose should know," punned Curly.

"No chocolate bar for you till noon for that," penalized Giggles.

The spirits of the three chums were noticeably higher. They had tried not to take their experiences too seriously, each for the other's sake, and it is well that they had for all three had been called upon to undergo repeated shocks of varying nature.

Resuming their progress, following their noses as instructed, creeping—sometimes crawling through the passageway—the chums came to an extremely small cavern, a slit or fissure where there appeared to be no ceiling. The cavern was narrow, circular in shape, with the passageway leading on, diagonally across, but the whole interior so narrow that it was impossible for flashlights to gauge the extent of the shadowy space above. The awesomeness of the place had its effect upon the chums. There was a "pressing in" feeling as though the circular wall would close upon them, silently, crushingly, until they were simply squeezed out of existence.

"Isn't this queer?" whispered Giggles.

But before either Bing or Curly could answer back, a voice strangely like Giggles' had whispered, *"Isn't this queer?"*

"Gee—this is fierce!" moaned Bing, starting in alarm.

"Gee—this is fierce!" moaned a voice.

"I wonder what it is?" gasped Curly.

"I wonder what it is?" the darkness gasped in return.

"It's some sort of a crazy echo!" said Giggles, and waited for his words to be repeated.

But they weren't!

"Oh, gee!" exclaimed Bing, bewildered. "Doesn't an echo always work?"

"I—I guess so," admitted Giggles, teeth chattering. "M-m-maybe it wasn't an echo after all!"

"But what was it, then?" asked Curly, tremulously. "Say—things are getting worse and worse!"

CHAPTER VIII

HELPLESS PRISONERS

A FAINT flicker of light which looked suspiciously as though it were cast by one of the circus torches, shone through from the passageway across the circular room. Instinctively the three chums pulled back as they heard footsteps and the booming voice of the white chieftain.

"We got the door open all right. Don't see nothin', though. Let 'er go again, Redwood!"

"Ow . . . oooooh!"

The blood-curdling cry, followed by a moment of tense silence, as the chums shrunk back in the shadows.

"Nope. I don't hear nothin', not a sound!"

"Big echo . . . heap, big echo somewhere!" insisted Redwood. "Echo tell where treasure is."

Giggles, Bing and Curly pinched each other.

"They're coming in here!" whispered Bing. "We'd better . . ."

"No!" commanded Giggles. "Let 'em catch us!"

"*What?*"

The white chieftain was the first one to enter the peculiar-shaped room. He stamped about with a heavy, swaggering stride, gazing up at the cavernous space above. He was followed by Redwood and then by the huge frame of the colored giant who bent low as he pushed a blazing torch in ahead of him. What a terrible looking trio! All three reminding the boys of savage beasts in a lair, restless, roaming, roaring. It was the gleaming stare of the colored giant which discovered them.

"Ha! Ha! Ha!" laughed the black man. "So here yo' is!"

"Tee, hee, hee!" giggled Giggles. "Here we *is*, is right!"

The white chieftain whirled about in astonishment. So did Redwood. Bing and Curly straightened up, defiantly. The colored giant moved over to bring the light from the torch full upon them.

"Well, where in thunder did you fellers come from?"

"Through that passageway there," answered Giggles, with a silencing gesture toward Bing and Curly. "We want to get out of this place. We've seen enough. *We're through!*"

"What d'ya mean, you've seen enough? You're through?"

"Boys know something," intimated Redwood. "Boys know cave . . . else boys no get out bat room! Never! Never! Blue Eagle say, my gran'father say bats mean death. E. B.—he feed Injuns to bats—sky full of bats. I not go near room, not for million dollar—two million dollar!"

"Heap brave Injun, you are!" sniffed the white

chieftain in disgust. "So superstitious you're goin' around with your fingers crossed!"

"Ha! Ha! Ha!" bellowed the colored giant, rocking on his heels.

"Pipe down! You can't say nothin'!" snapped the big hulk of a white man, turning upon the black Goliath who backed up, humbly and apologetically. There was no mistaking who was in authority, and that the authority was respected.

"All right, boss, all right. Yo' all don't haf to take mah head off!"

The white chieftain stalked over and peered into the passageway through which the chums had come. He sniffed at the air and turned back to glare at the boys, questioningly.

"Put your hands up over your heads!" he ordered.

The three chums complied, Curly holding his ax aloft.

"I'll take the hatchet, George," said the burly leader, enjoying his little joke. "We can't let you chop down no more cherry trees!"

Then the white chieftain frisked Curly's pockets with his big hands, slapping Curly heavily on the hips and jostling him about roughly. He uncovered the daggers with a growl of surprise, and tossed them over to Redwood. Curly's pockets yielded very little, however . . . a knife, a key ring, a metal matchbox, a can opener, a large kerchief, the stub of a pencil, and, of course, the flashlight.

Bing was next. He surrendered his flashlight

first, then the daggers, three of them, and the contents of his pockets—a quarter and two nickels, a jackknife, a small mirror, a comb, a cake of soap, a handkerchief and several nails.

"Ho, ho! You're a pretty boy, ain't you?" jeered the white chieftain, holding up the cake of soap, mirror and comb.

Bing grinned nervously but made no reply. The white chieftain moved over to Giggles.

"Well, what have you got? More daggers!"

The leader made a jab at Giggles' waist.

"Tee, hee, hee!" giggled Giggles, and bent double. "Stop it!"

"Straighten up here. What's the matter with you?" The white chieftain cuffed Giggles across the face with the flat of his hand. "No monkey business, see!"

"But you're tickling me!" protested Giggles, as hands were again laid upon him. "I can't stand it. Ow . . . ow . . . tee, hee, hee!"

Once more Giggles bent double, dropping his arms to pull at his shirt front convulsively.

"Say! I'll lay you out if you pull that again!"

Bing and Curly looked on, alarmed. There was little mercy in the white chieftain's face. He was a bad egg to fool with. Giggles had better be careful. What ailed him anyway? Had he gone daffy?

Giggles gained control of himself with an effort, stiffening to permit a continuance of the search. He, too, had a jackknife, some small coins, a matchbox, a flashlight, a handkerchief, some rifle bullets, and, woe of woes—a bar of chocolate!

Bing and Curly caught their breaths. *Where* was the piece of the map? Giggles shot them a quick, implying look. And, in that moment, they understood. Dumbly now, they watched the expression of appetizing joy on the white leader's face as he peeled the wrapper from the chocolate bar and held it up so that his two consorts could see.

"Candy!"

Redwood and the colored giant advanced, hungrily. The white chieftain broke off two chunks of equal size.

"Here, George!" he tossed a chunk to the black man. "It's a different George this time, son," he added, turning to bow mockingly at Curly. "There you are, Redwood. That's the way I splits the spoils with them as is with me. Now I'm savin' a lick for Tiny Thumb. Much obliged, boys, for the nourishment. We were kind o' late for our breakfast this mornin'!"

"Don't mention it!" replied Giggles, while Bing and Curly glared. "We just had a good dinner . . . last evening!"

It was misery, watching that chocolate bar disappear, especially after having counted on it for so long. But Bing and Curly followed Giggles' cue and pretended not to mind in the least.

"Now," said the white chieftain, smacking his lips in better humor, "I'm troublin' you boys to come along with us like good fellers . . . and as long as you act sensible, I acts sensible. I'm a fair-minded man, I am, but I don't stand for no monkey business. Ain't that so, George?"

"It sho' am, boss. It sho' am!"

"All we want is to get out of this place," reiterated Giggles. "We're through!"

The white chieftain laughed.

"Well, I wouldn't say you was exactly through, cuz you're goin' to help us out considerable. But if you acts sensible, you ain't goin' to get hurt. Get on ahead of us now and don't make no break to get away." He tapped a hip pocket threateningly. "If you do, I got a little *colt* back here that's liable to chase you!"

The boys stumbled into the passageway as directed, groping along in the flickering gleam of the torch which was sputtering low. The further they went, the smaller the passageway grew. Finally they came to the door that the white chieftain had referred to, a wooden door, this time, which had been fitted into the rock threshold, effectively sealing the entrance. The door was swung back so that the boys could look beyond into a larger passageway. But Giggles, in the lead, was moved to push the door half-shut, the door swinging noiselessly. As he did so, he pointed excitedly to a drawing on the upper panel, the drawing of an Indian with hand to his mouth as though in the act of giving a war whoop, and, facing this Indian across what appeared to be a gap, stood another Indian in the same pose. Beneath this crude drawing was the wording, in white letters as before:

IF YOU HEAR IT—YOU KNOW!

E. B.

Quickly, before their captors should discover this most significant of signs, Giggles swung the door back against the wall so that only its outside face was visible. Hearts leaping with hope and anxiety, the three chums felt their way out into the larger passage, stopping to await orders as to which direction to go. It was with great relief that they saw the white chieftain, the Indian and the colored giant pass heedlessly through the entrance, and join them —the black man reaching back with a long arm to pull the door shut after him, while he held the torch up with the other that they all might see what lay ahead of them, to the left.

"We're back-tracking!" whispered Giggles. "I'm sure of it! Not that we've ever been through this passageway before, but we must have missed seeing it when we went into that bats' cave!"

Giggles' sense of direction proved wonderfully accurate as was evidenced by the party's arrival, some ten minutes later, at the point where the passageway branched off. It had been the right spur of this main passageway that the boys had taken in their attempted escape. Now they realized that they were not far distant from the room where Uncle Eb had been confined.

"What did you let 'em catch us for?" asked Bing of Giggles, at the first opportunity.

"The map!" whispered Giggles. "We've got to get that map!"

"Shut up!" ordered the white chieftain, closing in. "I forgot to tell you birds. There'll be no openin' of your traps till you're spoken to from now on. An' that don't mean speakin' to each other either!"

Coming to the narrow slit in the wall, the chums paused. Inside they heard a familiar, low moaning. Uncle Eb! Then a squeaky voice.

"Cut your sobbing, Uncle. Cut your sobbing. You'd ought to be in the movies. You don't get nothing for your tears here. Except getting on my nerves. Cut it out now!"

"Where's the others gone?" asked Uncle Eb. "Where 'ave they gone? Take the chains off me! Take 'em off! I'll tell 'em. I'll tell 'em everythin'. My grandfather was crazy . . ."

"Sure, I don't doubt it," soothed the dwarf man, in an irritated tone. "I don't doubt it! For the love of P. T. Barnum, will you . . . ?"

There was a commotion at the entrance as the white chieftain forced Giggles, Bing and Curly into the room, single file.

"Boys!" screamed Uncle Eb again, hysterically. He tugged at the chains which held him to the wall.

Giggles started over toward Uncle Eb, sympathetically.

"Stay away!" ordered the little man whom the leader called Tiny Thumb. "Say, chief, I'm sure glad you're back!" he exclaimed. "I don't know who's the nutty one now, me or him!"

The chieftain stooped down, opening a large hand to reveal a smeary piece of chocolate.

"Here . . . don't say I never gave you nothin'!"

The dwarf took the sticky lump and shoved it in his mouth greedily. Then he held out his small hand again.

"Gimme some more!"

"Ha! Ha! Ha!" laughed the colored giant.

Even the three chums grinned.

The white chieftain, hands on hips, stared down at Tiny Thumb in amazement, then reached down, jerked him up and held him out at arms length.

"Why, you chesty little cuss!"

The dwarf man struggled but was powerless in the white man's iron grip. The muscles in the great arm, holding him, bulged and rippled. The chums, looking on, could not help wondering what would happen if a real clash should ever develop between the white chieftain and the colored giant who so seemingly held him in fear. Was the big seven footer actually afraid of the self-appointed ringleader or was he just awaiting his chance, pretending respect at present? Something in his attitude now, as he stood eyeing the white chieftain up and down with a glittering look, suggested . . . what *did* it suggest? No *good* for any one, at least!

"You're just a mouthful for an average-sized man!" taunted the leader. "And here you've the nerve to ask for another bite! . . . Where's that map?"

"It—it's over there, sir," answered the squeaky voice, submissively.

The white leader set the dwarf down.

"Get it!" he commanded.

The dwarf had stuck the map in a crevice of the cavern near a torch which had been placed at an angle to illuminate the room. The colored giant slouched over and jabbed his torch alongside as the dwarf pulled at the roll of parchment.

"Sit down, boys," invited the white chieftain, as Uncle Eb looked on, babbling to himself. 'Sorry we ain't got no chairs."

The chums dropped upon the floor obediently.

"Now I wants to ask you fellers a few questions," announced the white chieftain, taking up the map. "And I wants to get straight answers because the first bit of crooked work I runs into . . ." He drew a finger in a slit-like motion across his neck. "—you gets it right here, see?"

The chums saw; at least, they nodded.

"I'll tell! I'll tell!" cried Uncle Eb. "Take off these chains! Take . . . !"

"You keep still!" bellowed the ringleader, "that's

all you got to do. Keep still. You're not in on this cross-examination."

The white chieftain acted as though he particularly liked the sound of the last words. He cocked his head toward the boys and stuck out his pointed chin, snarling through his teeth.

"Crrrr-oss examina-shun! Did you hear?"

"Yes, sir," answered Giggles, politely.

"Shut up! Wait till I asks you a question, will ya?"

"Yes, sir!" said Giggles, with even greater politeness.

The white chieftain glowered.

"I said 'wait'!"

"But you *did* ask me a question!" insisted Giggles.

"Well, I meant a *real* one!" retorted the leader, a bit abashed. He wheeled about as he imagined a snicker from the colored giant. "What's that?"

"Nothin', boss, nothin'!" spoke the black man, quickly.

"We're a goin' to settle this here treasure question right this minute!" declared the white man, fingering the map. "Now, the first thing I wants to know is—has any of you boys ever seen this before?"

"Sure!" answered Giggles.

"Say 'sir' to me!" ordered the white chieftain. "This is just like a army court martial!"

"Oh, then it isn't a cross-examination, sir?" asked Giggles.

"No, it is . . . certainly! It's both, if I say so!"

"Yes, sir," swallowed Giggles, winking soberly at Bing and Curly who gazed at him aghast.

"So, you've lamped this map before, have ya?"

"How, sir?"

"You're not dumb. You've laid your eyes on . . ."

"*Oh!* Yes, sir!"

"In fact, you knows quite a bit about it, don't you?"

"Yes, sir."

"Ummm hmmmm!"

The white chieftain glanced at his confederates, immensely satisfied with the results he was obtaining from the cross-examination.

"Supposin' you tells me just how much you knows about this here map?"

"The upper left hand corner's torn off of it," answered Giggles, very promptly, as Bing and Curly gasped.

The white chieftain stared.

"That's so!" he said, impressed. Then, recollecting, "Wait a minute! You seen that when you was here before!"

"Did I?" asked Giggles, innocently. "Well, I couldn't have seen anything about the *echo cave* in it before . . . could I?"

This was a stunner. Redwood and the colored giant and the dwarf man looked their interest now.

They crowded about the three chums, attention riveted upon Giggles.

"Echo cave!" shouted the white chieftain, reaching down and yanking Giggles to his feet. "That's what we want to find out about! And you're goin' to show us . . . that's bein' sensible! We ain't goin' to hurt you so long as you're sensible!"

"I tell you . . . boys know something," repeated Redwood. "Boys know more'n that empty head over there." He nodded at Uncle Eb who had slumped over in a heap. "Anyhow, boys tell more . . . don't pay have empty head!"

"Here's the map!" said the white chieftain, excitedly thrusting the parchment into Giggles' hands. "You show us where the echo cave is and we'll let you go!"

Giggles took the map testily. His fingers trembled. He hoped that no one would notice it. Bing and Curly restrained their thumping nerves with difficulty. They knew that their chum had made a deliberate play for possession of the map, that he had flirted with the giving out of what appeared to be invaluable information, and that, if he didn't produce, now that he had gone this far . . . ? Well, they hadn't liked that neck-clicking warning of the white chieftain's a little bit!

"It'll take me a few minutes," countered Giggles, stalling for time.

"That's all right," assured the white chieftain. "I've had Redwood hollerin' his head off over the whole cave tryin' to locate that darn echo room. If you . . ."

"Oh, so that's what he was doing . . . that Ow. . . ooooh stuff?" asked Giggles, glancing up.

The Indian had enough of a sense of humor to smile.

"Much Ow . . . ooooh," he said. "No Ow . . . ooooh back!"

"Well, you give me a little while to go over this map and I'll promise you'll hear all the Ow . . . oooohs you want!" said Giggles.

"That's the boy!" encouraged the white chieftain.

Then, while Bing and Curly hardly dared breathe, Giggles sat down beside them and began tracing out the markings on the map as though he had not a worry in the world!

CHAPTER IX

A BATTLE OF WITS

TEN painful minutes crawled past.

At the end of that time, Giggles looked up soberly and asked, in a matter-of-fact voice:

"Got a pencil?"

The white chieftain fumbled in his pockets and brought out a stub of one. Giggles took it without further comment and bent over the map again, under the flicker of the torches and the gleaming stare of the peculiar quartet. Bing and Curly shifted their positions uneasily.

"Now for a little piece of paper!"

Giggles actually appeared to be growing excited. He had followed a rather crooked line with the pencil stub and had strengthened some of the faded tracings on the map.

"Here you be . . ." The white chieftain once more complied, crowding closer that he might follow Giggles' markings.

Eyeing the map shrewdly, Giggles made a number of dots on the paper, which chanced to be the back of a bill advertising Brockton's World's Greatest Shows. He then drew a snake-like line, taking great care to make it an accurate reproduction of a charted passageway. When he had finished he jumped to his feet with an enthusiastic exclamation.

"There!"

"You got her all figured out?" asked the white chieftain, eagerly.

"Just about," answered Giggles. "But you can't get far without Uncle Eb to help you. He knows this cave like a book. Don't let him kid you."

"Nobody kids *me!*" bellowed the white chieftain, glowering angrily toward the shackled hermit. "I'll . . ."

"Wait!" entreated Giggles, "you can't get anything out of him that way. The more you scare him the less he'll tell you. Why don't you let me talk to him?"

"You?"

"Sure. I know him. And you can't ever find that echo cave unless he shows you how. I might take you right to it and yet you couldn't tell you were there!"

The white chieftain glared at Giggles unbelievingly.

"What's that?"

"You see, echo cave doesn't always echo," explained Giggles. "I have my own idea about where it is . . . but there's a trick to it . . . and I'm dead certain Uncle Eb knows that trick!"

"Ummmm! Heap big trick!" agreed Redwood, nodding his head emphatically. "Boy right. My gran'father . . ."

"Never mind your grandfather now!" interrupted the white chieftain gruffly. "We got to be gettin' busy. Go to it, son. See what you can do with the old man. But no monkey-shines, remember! I ain't in no humor to be spoofed!"

Bing and Curly stood up nervously as Giggles, map in hand, sauntered over to the grizzled Uncle Eb. He knelt down beside the peculiar owner of the house on the bluff and said something to him in an undertone.

"I don't know! I don't know!" whimpered the old fellow. "Why don't they let me go?"

Giggles said something else in an undertone. Uncle Eb ceased his whimpering and looked up hopefully.

"Will you?" he asked, reaching out imploringly toward the white chieftain. "Will you let me go if I shows you where the echo cave is?"

"Absolute!" assured the ringleader, with a consulting glance at the colored giant, the dwarf and the Indian.

"Find echo cave . . . soon find treasure!" reiterated Redwood. "My gran'father . . ."

"Hang your grandfather!" exploded the white chieftain, impatiently. "All you been doin' is talk about your grandfather, but he ain't done nothin' for us since we got in this cave. 'Bout all he was good for was locatin' the map, but what good's the map even, if we can't make head nor tail of it?"

Redwood shrugged his shoulders.

"Map made so's to fool Indian. E.B. want treasure all to self. That's why he kill my gran'-father!"

There was bitterness in Redwood's words. He glared at Uncle Eb as he uttered them. But the hermit paid little heed. He was concerned, very much concerned, with something Giggles was whispering to him. As Giggles spoke, Uncle Eb took to nodding his head understandingly.

"See here . . . what you tellin' him?" demanded the white chieftain, suspiciously.

"I told him you'd let us all go if we could find echo cave for you," answered Giggles. "Is that so?"

The white chieftain hesitated. Bing and Curly, alert for the slightest move, saw the crafty Redwood wink.

"Yep, that's so. Show us echo cave and youse all can beat it. We won't need no help after that. Will we, Redwood?"

"My gran'father say before he die . . . 'treasure lie in straight line from echo cave. Straight as your nose,' he say," responded Redwood.

At the mention of "nose," Giggles, Bing and Curly exchanged significant glances.

"Well, how about it?" persisted Giggles. "Uncle Eb can't find the cave while he's tied to this wall."

"Take those chains off, George," ordered the white chieftain, thumbing a hand at the colored giant.

A clinking and clanking and Uncle Eb was freed.

The old fellow was shivering from cold and nervousness. He put out a hand to Giggles for support until he had stretched some of the kinks out of his legs.

"Better let me have a torch," suggested Giggles, as the party prepared to set out, "or else give me my flashlight back. Uncle Eb and I ought to go ahead."

The white chieftain considered.

"All right. Here's your light. Redwood, give George one o' them electric blazes . . . and use the other one yourself!"

"I no like. I take torch," mumbled Redwood, distastefully. He tossed Bing's flashlight to the colored giant who examined it curiously, grinning with pleasure. The other flashlight he gave to Tiny Thumb. This done, the Indian went to the crevice in the wall supporting a half-burned torch, and tore the torch from its fastening. "Me ready," he said.

The white chieftain nodded at Giggles meaningly.

"We're all ready," he said, "and heaven help you if you don't show us where that echo cave is!"

Giggles made no answer but led the way through the narrow slit to the passageway beyond. Bing and Curly were feeling a trifle easier now although they were at a loss to know what Giggles had up his sleeve. Their chum had wisely paid no attention to them in his debating over the map. He had apparently thrown his entire interest on the side of the white chieftain. At least, the white chieftain had

been sufficiently impressed to follow Giggles' suggestions. Bing and Curly quietly rejoiced at the
thoughts of Uncle Eb being free. So far so good.
But what was that intrepid Giggles going to do
next? He was basking in the good graces of the
white chieftain now—they all were, for that matter
—but basking in the good graces of such an individual was an exceedingly uncomfortable experience.
If only Giggles would be able to engineer things
through to the finish without stirring up the wrath
of the strange four in whose power they were!
Bing and Curly could tell that Giggles was even
now concocting a plan—a desperate plan, perhaps.
Just what course this plan would take the boys had
not the slightest idea. All they could do was to
follow along, keeping their eyes fixed upon Giggles
for the least possible sign.

"I'll take the map, thank you!" said the white
chieftain, as the party reached the passageway.

"Sure," obliged Giggles, handing the map back
promptly. "All I need is this outline I made." He
pointed to the rumpled circus bill on the back of
which he had drawn.

"Hey, you're goin' right back the way we came
from!" protested the white chieftain, in surprise.

"Sure," admitted Giggles, with unconcern. "But
we know where we're going, don't we, Uncle?"

"Echo cave!" said Uncle Eb, simply. "That's
where we're goin'!"

"I told you him know something," reminded Redwood, "I told you."

"You told me nothin'!" snapped the white chieftain. "It's lucky for you that you even remembered what your grandfather said about the treasure . . . and the map . . ."

Redwood's brow knotted.

"You think . . . cuz we find echo cave soon . . . then treasure . . . you make fun my gran'father, eh? You think can tell Redwood 'ha ha' . . . what's he done? . . . eh?"

The white chieftain laughed in what, to the boys, seemed like an obvious attempt to cover up his real intentions.

"Naw . . . none o' that, Redwood. None o' that. But you know, right down in your redskin soul, that it's me, the guy who's gettin' this treasure for you! You wouldn't never have tackled this here deal alone. And where'd you got, if you had, without my brain?"

"Ha! Ha! Ha!" boomed a voice from behind. " 'Scuse me, boss . . . *your brain!*"

There was more than the idle jest in this taunt and the white chieftain sensed it for he wheeled about to glare savagely at the towering black man who returned the look with eyes which gleamed a cold white in the flickering light.

"Gee!" whispered Bing to Curly, "they're beginning to fight over something they haven't got, already!"

"Hope they do!" murmured Curly, in a tremulous undertone, "it would sure help us!"

There was no uncertainty in the actions of either Giggles or Uncle Eb. Both seemed to know exactly where they were going. True, Giggles kept a step or two in the lead so that all Uncle Eb had to do was to tag along with the white chieftain and Redwood at his heels, Bing and Curly coming next, and the colored giant and the dwarf man bringing up the rear as a sort of guard. A peculiar looking outfit all the way around, any one would have thought, could they have seen.

Presently Giggles stopped in front of the door which led into the small, circular cavern where they had been discovered more than an hour before.

"What's the grand idee?" asked the white chieftain, "we been in there already. Redwood's hollered in there, too. No echo."

"Maybe there wasn't," assented Giggles, "but there was a reason. Uncle Eb'll fix that. Now just you let us go in first!"

Giggles put his weight against the door.

"Hold on! What's that?"

From down the passageway came a low, quivering whine. The whine was repeated as the party stood, wondering. Then the whine, growing louder, suddenly changed into an excited barking.

"Spot!" cried Giggles, Bing and Curly together.

Uttering a cry of joy as flashlights were turned in the direction of the bow wows, Uncle Eb stumbled forward to greet his faithful dog. Spot bounded into view, dragging a short piece of rope.

"Well, well, partner! Glad to see you. Glad to see you!" cried the owner of the house on the bluff. "You're a brave dog, a very brave dog!"

"Forget the dog!" ordered the white chieftain, "unless you want the purp knocked off. We should o' done that in the first place. *Show us that echo cave!*"

"Yes, sir," answered Uncle Eb, meekly, *"yes, sir!"*

The door gave under Giggles' increasing pressure and Uncle Eb followed him in, Spot leaping at his heels.

"Wait there . . . the rest of you," ordered Giggles.

"Nothin' stirrin'. . . I'm comin' in with you!" said the white chieftain. "You birds is not goin' to git out o' my sight!"

"Tee, hee, hee!" giggled Giggles. "Come on, then . . . if that's what's worrying you."

The burly ringleader came. And he saw to it that his three strange companions came, too, with the colored giant pushing Bing and Curly in. It was slow going through the low ceilinged passageway until the party emerged into the small, circular room with its seemingly endless space overhead. Here, Giggles—in the lead—stooped down quickly and picked up a crumpled piece of parchment paper, stuffing it inside his shirt. The action went unnoticed by all, save Uncle Eb, for which Giggles was exceedingly thankful. He flashed his light overhead and pretended an interest in the cavernous regions above.

"How's she look?" he asked of Uncle Eb.

"Ummm!" said Uncle Eb, gazing studyingly aloft. "She's the place all right. Now let's see . . ."

He looked about him, walking around the circular room close to the wall several times, with the white chieftain watching curiously, hands on hips. Spot trailed his master, sniffing at Uncle Eb's heels. But Uncle Eb had eyes for more than the interior of the room. He was sizing up the position of the white chieftain, Redwood, the colored giant and the dwarf man.

"If it's just the same to you, would you mind a movin' away from that openin' there?" Uncle Eb asked, finally. "This here echo is hard to make . . . and everythin's got to be just right."

Bing and Curly stepped to one side at once. Redwood and the colored giant eyed the white chieftain consultingly before they moved.

"Give the old boy a chance," ordered the ringleader. "If he doesn't come through this time he's a goner!"

"He'll come through all right," guaranteed Giggles. "Didn't I tell you he knew this cave like a book?"

"We've been told lots of things," said the white chieftain dubiously. "We has to be showed now!"

"I'll show you!" assured Uncle Eb, his voice trembling excitedly. "I'll show you! My grandfather was crazy, but I'll show you!"

The white chieftain flashed a disgusted glance at Redwood.

"Between your grandfather and his'n there ain't much choice!" he growled. "You're both daffy on grandfathers! Come on over here and get out of the geezer's way. He may be a claimin' you're standin' on the echo if you don't!"

The three chums grinned. Redwood and the colored giant sauntered over to the far side of the circular room near the small opening which led into the weird cavern of the bats. Giggles shuddered from a glance at it. Bats! Would he ever forget that clammy experience? Chances were he wouldn't, or Bing and Curly either. But now they were in a different sort of a predicament, fast approaching a crisis. The situation was not so repelling, even though it was more fraught with a threat of danger. In the next few seconds every move would have to be carefully timed. Giggles hoped that Uncle Eb would be equal to the occasion. He had been forced to explain his plan hurriedly when he had talked to Uncle Eb in an undertone while the old fellow was still shackled to the wall. So far Uncle Eb had played his part magnificently, proof positive to Giggles that he was not as dumb or as scared as he had made out to be when there had appeared no hope of escape. Now his grizzled face looked almost fiendish as he watched his enemies take their new positions. Only Tiny Thumb had not moved. He stood quietly beside Bing and Curly to the right of the entrance to the circular room from the recently traversed passageway. Giggles edged over toward that same entrance. Spot dropped down on the stone floor, tongue hanging out, eyes dancing, wondering what this solemn affair was all about, and wanting a chance to josh the boys—dog fashion—on his being able to get away from the place where they had tied him. Just now Spot felt like a second Houdini. And no one had given him any credit for his exploit. Poor, innocent Spot, not to have appreciated that his master and the boys were, at that very moment, trying to accomplish a Houdini themselves! A get-away without revealing the hidden secret of the echo room! Could they?

Apparently they couldn't. With a sober glance at Giggles, Uncle Eb took the first bold step. He turned to Tiny Thumb.

"Say, you—you was the last one in here, wasn't you?"

The dwarf man nodded.

"Well, did you shut the door after you?"

A moment's reflection, then another nod of the head . . . a negative nod. The owner of the house on the bluff swung about to address the white chieftain appealingly.

"That door's got to be closed. There can't be no echo till she's shut tight. That's the whole thin'!"

"Shut the door!" bawled the ringleader, impatiently.

"Get ready to try out your 'Ow . . . ooooh' again," said Giggles to Redwood. "You'll hear her come back to you this time."

Redwood stiffened expectantly as Tiny Thumb disappeared in the passageway, all eyes turning toward the entrance.

"There's a regular sound box in here when the door's closed, is that it, Uncle?" asked Giggles, by way of suggesting an explanation.

"Voice can't get out . . . voice got to come back," Uncle Eb replied.

"Sounds reasonable," opined the white chieftain, with pleased anticipation. "Got that door shut, Tiny?"

"No . . . not yet . . . she sticks!" panted the dwarf man from the passageway.

"I'll fix it," volunteered Uncle Eb. He was gone before the white chieftain could bid him otherwise. And Spot was with him.

"All right?" called the white chieftain after a few minutes' wait in which the gasping of the dwarf was plainly heard.

"All right!" answered Uncle Eb. "Try it!"

Redwood drew in a deep breath. Then he let forth the murderous cry which had struck such fear and awe in the hearts of Giggles, Bing and Curly before they had been able to determine what it was or from whence it had come. There was the slightest second of silence, just enough for Redwood to catch his breath, when, from the spacious black regions above, the blood-curdling "Ow . . . ooooh!" came reverberating back. The white chieftain, Redwood and the colored giant stared upwards, spellbound, and, as they did so, three forms shot, like streaks of summer lightning, for the entrance!

Everything had happened so suddenly that the captors of Giggles, Bing and Curly were caught completely off guard. Their joyous amazement at the discovery of the echo room had hardly been kindled than they were treated to the spectacle of three flying figures. Bing and Curly had acted upon Giggles' warning signal instantaneously, unquestioningly. And they were through the passageway, and the door, again open, almost before any one had started in pursuit.

"To the right!" directed Giggles, bringing up the rear, and using his flashlight to advantage.

"Where's Uncle Eb?" cried Bing. "And the dwarf?"

"I don't know where the dwarf is!" answered Giggles. "We should fret about him. Uncle Eb's up ahead somewhere. Come on! Get going!"

Giggles pulled the heavy wooden door shut after him with a wrenching tug. Then he set off after his two chums on a continuation of the passageway beyond which they had never gone before!

"Where are we going?" asked Curly, frenziedly.

"We're going to find the treasure!" snapped Giggles, "where'd you suppose?"

"I thought you said you wanted to get out of here? That we were through!"

"Well, a fellow can change his mind, can't he . . . after getting away from those guys?"

"Yes, but . . . !"

"Don't argue. Keep going! We can't afford to get caught again!"

There was a battering sound behind . . . and mad yells. The three chums hurried on, coming to an abrupt left turn and following around it, clambering over large rock formations, falling, stumbling, but pressing forward.

"What was the idea of making a break for it, anyway?" grumbled Bing. "The big boy said he'd let us go if we showed him the echo room."

"Don't you believe it!" scoffed Giggles. "He's as crooked as a seven jointed stove pipe!"

"Look! There's Uncle Eb!" exclaimed Curly, as Giggles' flashlight caught some figures in front.

"And will you look who he's got with him!" howled Bing, astounded.

"The dwarf!" cried Giggles. "Tee, hee, hee! Can you beat that?"

Uncle Eb, hearing the boys, gave a glance back over his shoulder, and waved his free hand. The other hand and arm clutched the midget around the waist. Tiny Thumb was kicking furiously and making a frantic effort to get away but all to no avail.

The grizzled old hermit still had a powerful grip in his arms and the dwarf was not much of a load.

Now the chums found themselves in another great room which divided itself into many sections. This made them feel that they could slacken their pace in safety.

"Uncle Eb, you're a peach!" called Giggles when the chums had about caught up to him. "You got us out of that scrape fine!"

Uncle Eb's eyes sparkled. He set the dwarf down, retaining a hold on him, however.

"*I* got you out of the scrape? Say, son, don't you try to kid an old man like me. Uncle Eb just does as he's told, and mighty glad to do that. Uncle Eb ain't forgettin' either. If we gets out of this mess he's goin' to do somethin' for you boys, somethin' big!"

"Well, never mind about that," said Giggles, embarrassed. "We're having a good time! But what're you going to do with 'sawed off' there?"

Uncle Eb looked down at the scowling dwarf and shook the little fellow playfully.

"Ain't he cute?" the owner of the house on the bluff chuckled. "He looked so darn ornamental I just couldn't resist totin' him along. Besides, it just all of a sudden struck me he might turn out useful. Can't never tell, you know. I'd a lot rather have him with us than, well—agin us! And that's what he'd kept on bein' if I'd left him with them!"

"Great!" exclaimed Giggles, with enthusiasm.

"This gives us a chance to hold a nice little cross-examination all our own, too! We ought to find out a few interesting things from Tiny."

"You won't get nothing from me!" snapped the dwarf, in a high, shrill voice.

"Won't we?" rejoined Giggles, equally defiant. "We'll see!"

CHAPTER X

FIGURING THINGS OUT

BY the time the white chieftain and his two husky cronies, George and Redwood, reached the outer passageway there was not a visible trace of the fleeing boys. But there was no doubt in the white chieftain's mind as to the direction that the fugitives had gone. He stood a moment, big hands opening and closing in fury as he muttered an exclamation of disgust at himself.

"Might have knowed better!" he said. "Well, they ain't really got away yet. Say, *where's Tiny Thumb?*"

Redwood and the colored giant peered about, using a torch and flashlight.

"Him gone, too," announced the Indian, bluntly.

"Ha! Ha! Ha!" laughed the colored giant, flashing a row of dazzling white teeth. "Boss, yo' sho' am easy!"

"Easy nothin'!" snapped the white chieftain. "I had the kids scared green. We found the echo cave, didn't we?"

"Yas-suh, we sho' foun' dat!"

"Kids no fool," opined Redwood, soberly. "Old man no fool either. Only act like one some time. Old man pick Tiny Thumb up. Run off with him."

"What do we care?" countered the white chieftain. "What we're after is the treasure. Them boys can't interfere none. We'll like as not run into 'em again, too. Didn't they get away from us once and we caught 'em? Besides, they don't know where the treasure is. *We got the map!*"

The white chieftain tapped the rolled parchment with the back of his hand.

"You sez to me all along, find you the echo room and you find the treasure. All right. Now we're not a goin' to worry about nobody gettin' away. What we're goin' to do is make a bee line for the place where that treasure is . . . a bee line, understand? I ain't hankerin' to stay down here much longer!"

"Me either, boss . . . me either!" emphasized the colored giant. "Do yo' stuff, Redwood. Do yo' stuff!"

The Indian reached out for the map gravely, handing the torch to the white chieftain in exchange for the parchment. Carefully, Redwood unrolled the faded paper.

"Too bad Tiny Thumb not here," he said, shaking his head. "Tiny Thumb know lot about maps."

"Yeah," rejoined the white chieftain, dryly. "Everybody knows a lot about everythin', but you. You're not so dumb yourself. Get busy! What's that you was sayin' about your grandfather's nose?"

The Indian registered a look of disgust.

"No say anythin' 'bout gran'father's nose. Say

gran'father say . . . treasure lie in straight line
from echo cave . . . straight as your nose. . . ."

"Ha! Ha! Ha!" roared the colored giant,
again. "His nose ain't straight. It's crooked. You
cain't find no treasure dat-a-way!"

"Shut up!" ordered the white chieftain, irritably.

"Here echo cave on map," pointed out Redwood.
"We come here . . . and here . . . and here . . .
see?"

The white chieftain and the colored giant pushed
forward to glance over Redwood's shoulder.

While the three hardened characters were striv-
ing to make head and tail of the peculiar map which
bore no captions to explain the possible location of
various important points, Giggles, Bing and Curly
—aided by Uncle Eb—were trying just as desperately to figure things out for themselves. An attempt to get Tiny Thumb to talk had failed and
Giggles had temporarily abandoned the effort to
gain information from the dwarf while he sought
to piece together certain facts which might enable
them all to make their way to the treasure room.
As a precaution, however, before the conference was
begun, the rope was removed from Spot and used
to bind the dwarf who did promise to keep still
rather than suffer being gagged. On the short journey that he had been forced to take with Uncle Eb,
Tiny Thumb had almost been strangled because of
the old fellow's fear that the dwarf would cry out
and thus thwart the boys' chances for escape.

"First of all," said Giggles, when the dwarf had been placed out of hearing and Bing and Curly had gathered in a squatting semicircle about the grizzled Uncle Eb, "I think you ought to tell us everything you know about this treasure, Uncle. And the cave, too!"

Uncle Eb reached out a gnarled, bony hand to pet Spot. It was some moments before he spoke. Bing kept the flashlight, which had been recaptured from Tiny Thumb by Uncle Eb, playing its rays on the floor in front of them. Giggles looked down at his wrist watch. Fifteen minutes to eight! Wow, he was hungry, and thirsty. But—so were they all! Bing and Curly communicated with Giggles silently. This was a time when even hunger and thirst must be pushed in the background. It seemed as though they had been in the cave for days instead of only about six hours—since two o'clock that morning. But so very much had happened in those hours, and so very much more might still happen!

"All right, boys," said Uncle Eb, finally, "I'll tell you all I knows, which ain't much."

Giggles, Bing and Curly looked their surprise.

"Maybe you heard me a tellin' that big fellah that was a threatenin' me, a tellin' him that I didn't know nothin' about that map, and that I didn't know nothin' about any treasure. Maybe you thought I was a spoofin'. I wouldn't o' blamed you none. But facts is facts. Boys, just as sure as Uncle Eb sits here and draws breath, you knows just as much about that map and this here treasure that them men raves over, you knows just as much about it as I does. Maybe you knows more!"

Giggles eyed Uncle Eb shrewdly. It did seem as though the owner of the house on the bluff must be fabricating—covering up a mystery that he did not wish to impart to a soul. But, Giggles was forced to admit to himself, if Uncle Eb *was* falsifying, he certainly was putting on a sincerely sober face while doing it.

"You don't believe me?" asked Uncle Eb, his voice quavering piteously. "You don't believe me, *now?*" He made a pathetic, disappointed gesture with his hands as Spot, sensing his master's dejection, whined dolefully. "Nobody believes old Uncle Eb, Spot. Nobody!"

"We haven't said we didn't believe you," sympathized Giggles. "But it *is* a lot for anybody to swallow, that you lived in that house all these years, and yet never knew a thing about the treasure, or the map!"

"Boys so help me—the son of a truthful sailor— I never even knew there was a cave under my house!"

"WHAT?" exclaimed the three chums together, incredulously.

"Oh, yes . . . I'm crazy," cried the old hermit, as Spot cringed against his knees, understandingly. "That's the only answer. I'm crazy!" He put trembling hands to his temples and shook his head from side to side. "But you boys never saw my grandfather. He was crazy, too. A terrible man! I was afraid of him, I was. I still am!" Uncle Eb glanced about him fearsomely at the weird shadows in the cavernous room. The boys could almost feel the presence of something uncanny, the atmosphere of the place was so creepy, so unnerving.

"If he has treasure buried here I must save it! I can't let anybody get it. That's what he wanted me to stay here and guard the place for. To keep anybody from ever getting the treasure. That's it! That's it! What's the matter with Uncle Eb? That's it!"

Giggles tried his best to calm the old man who seemed to be given to fits of frenzy as well as moments of strange composure. But Uncle Eb, now that his tongue had been loosened, would go on.

"My grandfather never told me he had treasure hidden here. He was a close-mouthed man, he was! Nobody ever asked him any question about him or his affairs. They just did as he told 'em to, and they did it right quick. My own father was scared to death of him. He ran away so's he could get out of his power. But my grandfather followed him, and kept makin' life miserable for him, even after my father had settled down at Alpena and gotten married, and . . . and quit sailin' that lumber schooner for the Great Lakes Lumber Company. Oh, my father was an honorable man, he was. At least that's what he tried to be. Many's the time he'd told me wild tales about my grandfather before

I ever set eyes on the man. And me, a boy, just as scared of my father's father as my father was! Maybe worse. 'He's the terror of the Great Lakes,' my father tells me. 'Folks as knows him gives him everythin' he wants just to be let alone. And I've been afeared he would come and get hold of you and take you away with him. He'd do that to sort of even thin's up with me. If he does, all I can say is, don't cross him anywhere. Blood ties don't mean nothin' to him. He'd just as soon take your head off as the next fellah's. Home? He ain't got no home. Here I been his son and I couldn't tell you where he lives. On the lakes, I guess. Remember, son, if you ever runs into old Ebenezer Beecher, take it careful. There's no use tryin' to get away cuz he knows this whole country inside out. Best you can do is take your medicine and thank your stars you're still livin'.' "

Uncle Eb paused to gaze upon three exceedingly tense faces. His narrative had possessed gripping interest for Giggles, Bing and Curly, amazing as it was. The boys were trying hard to picture the type of character that Uncle Eb had described in the person of his grandfather, and to appreciate just how this early king of the then Michigan wilds, had exerted such a tremendous influence over all with whom he had come in contact.

"Go on," invited Giggles. "How'd you ever get in touch with your grandfather? Did he come and get you the way your father feared?"

"That he did!" answered Uncle Eb, and the boys thought they perceived a shudder pass through the old hermit's frame. "But not till after my mother had died of the typhoid and my father had lost his life in the big timber fire, leavin' me alone, a lad o' seventeen years, in the care o' settlers."

Spot yawned, and stretched himself out, after the manner of a dog who was just a trifle bored from the narration of facts with which he was familiar. The boys stirred uneasily and looked about.

"This is awful interesting," broke in Giggles. "But I don't see as it has much bearing on the fix we're in now. I thought maybe it might; that's why I asked you to tell us. Perhaps you'd better wait till some other time. If you want to keep any one from getting at that treasure, we'd better find it first!"

"I'm most through," explained Uncle Eb, not to be side-tracked. "So it ain't goin' to hurt nothin' to finish. I spent fifteen years on the Great Lakes with my grandfather a mixin' with the strangest crew that ever swopped oaths on one sailin' vessel. And in all that time I don't hardly set foot on land except when we come to this house, and then I'm one of the few what is ever allowed in it from off the ship. We is always goin' somewhere at night, and my grandfather and part o' the crew is goin' ashore, and comin' back just before dawn with a boat full of stuff. I don't dare ask what it's all about but I'm given to understand my grandfather's a trader

—a big merchantman what does business in lots of ports. I seen men flogged till they took sick and died in them days, and I wasn't hankerin' to meddle with what my grandfather was really doin'. Honest, I've heard Indians, and half-breeds, and the toughest kind of salts tellin' what they was a goin' to do to my grandfather; and I've wished many times that they'd do it too, but they always lost their nerve. They was just as much afeared o' him dead as they was alive. Maybe more! He was a he devil, that man!"

"Say, Giggles," called Bing, nervously. "We can't listen to Uncle Eb any longer. It isn't safe! Supposing . . ."

Giggles nodded and interceded once more.

"Uncle, you've just got to stop. We'll hear all about that later. Just now we—"

"I'm most through!" insisted Uncle Eb, emphatically. "I ain't told nobody about this—never! And right here's where there's maybe somethin' that'll help you out. My grandfather gets a bad stab wound one night when he's ashore and they bring him aboard ship in a bad way. We're miles off from the house on the bluff and it's rough weather, but he orders 'em to set sail at onc't and we makes the voyage in the teeth o' a whizzin' northwester. We has to wait till she calms considerable before we can lay to under the bluff; and then they gets the hoist device that they has runnin' up to that long window lookin' over the lake; and then they send me a old Indian that is my grandfather's right hand man—"

"Redwood's grandfather!" surmised Curly, pinching Giggles' arm.

"Sssh!" warned Giggles, in a low voice, "He's telling us something now!"

". . . They sends us up the hoist into the house and we fixes thin's so my grandfather can be sent up next. If you was down by the water line on the bluff you could see iron rings where the ship used to tie up. Well, we sends the hoist down and gets my grandfather in it—crippled like he is—and when we gets him about a hundred feet clear of the water, so's he danglin' in the air, and while we're lookin' out the window as he's comin' up, there's a terrific explosion below and the boat breaks in two pieces. And there's a tremendous flash of water, and the whole bluff shakes like an earthquake, and a cloud of dark smoke rolls up that covers my grandfather. And when it clears away all I can see is wreckage. And big waves splashin' up against the bluff, and bodies, and the Indian grinnin' from ear to ear, and pullin' up the hoist as quick as he can, and helpin' my grandfather in—through the window. . . ."

"Gee!" exclaimed Giggles, feeling a chilled sensation shoot through him. Bing and Curly bit their lips.

"I never knowed, but I had my suspicions," continued Uncle Eb, eyes gleaming. The old hermit reached out a bony hand to clutch Giggles' arm as his voice lowered and became husky with emotion. "The next night my grandfather and the Indian had a set to over somethin', and my grandfather killed him. I'm tellin' you, boys, you never seen a man like my grandfather, a match for man or beast when he was almost down on his back! He rallied after that, got so he could crawl around, and one day he takes the Indian's body and shows me the secret door to the basement, and tells me to stay behind and watch the place while he's gone. And he disappears down them stone steps, and he's gone for two days! I'm just about crazy from waitin' and wonderin' when he comes back, weak and out of his head, and jabberin' about the folks that was tryin' to get him, and laughin' about them not bein' able to do it. For the next six weeks he is a livin' ghost, makin' me wait on him hand and foot, and tellin' me what he'll do to me if I don't do everythin' he says. Oh, that may sound funny to you—that old Uncle Eb should be afeared of a body like that. But you ain't never knowed my grandfather, boys, and you ain't in no position to judge. He gets me to promise that I won't ever leave the premises, 'ceptin' to go to Bean Blossom for supplies, and that I'm to keep everybody out of the house—no matter who. I don't know what makes me promise that unless I'm kind of affected like, but I ain't dared break that promise to this day. And then, just before he dies. . . ."

Uncle Eb's voice dropped to a hoarse whisper and

he glanced about him nervously as though half expecting to see the shade of old Ebenezer Beecher appear menacingly before him.

". . . Just before he dies, he gives me a bag full of silver and gold pieces, and tells me to never—if I values my life—go down in that basement. But he makes sure that I knows where the key to that secret door is . . . and . . . and he shows me just inside the door where he has fixed a place for to . . . to hang his own body!"

"Tee, hee, hee!" giggled Giggles, but it was not a giggle of amusement; it was more a hysterical gasp of relief. He could not have held in longer without giving vent to some outburst. Bing and Curly found themselves on a similar nervous edge. How well they all remembered the blood-chilling sight of old Ebenezer Beecher's skeleton and the ominous wording above it:

WOE UNTO HIM WHO PASSES BENEATH MY BONES

E. B.

And here they were, penetrated far into the underground fastnesses of the great cave—all forbidden territory—if Ebenezer's threat was still to be regarded as law. What a character to have held sway over an individual like Uncle Eb for years following his departure into the Great Beyond! And now this same direful influence was communicating itself to the boys; every shadow was beginning to take on a hideous form; the damp, cool air in the cavern was changing to the ghastly breath of an unseen being. . . .

"Don't . . . don't go any further. We can guess the rest!" cried Giggles, as Uncle Eb bent his head and drew a deep sob. "For some reason that even you don't understand, your grandfather wanted to keep whatever treasure he has hidden, away from any one who might ever lay claim to it. And to be doubly sure of accomplishing this, he took care not even to tell you, his own grandson, about the treasure, or the map. You didn't even know as much about these things as the people whom your grandfather was protecting himself against. All he cared was to make certain that you guarded his house on the bluff—guarded it against intrusion. It was a sort of fiendish game with him, and it didn't make any difference to him whether you were the goat or not. Anything to get his end!"

"That's it! That's it!" sobbed Uncle Eb, happily. "You've got it, boy. I see it all now. It's been a gettin' clearer to me as I been a tellin' you, and piecin' together what's been a happenin'. If there's a treasure I wants it. It's a comin' to me if it's a comin' to anybody, and I guess I can't be blamed for gettin' down into this here cave when I didn't come o' my own free will . . . would you think so, boys?"

Giggles, Bing and Curly each assured Uncle Eb that they did not see how his grandfather could have taken offense at this latest development. Surely Uncle Eb had remained true to the dictates laid down for him all these years . . . and now that the fight had been carried well within the stronghold itself, Ebenezer Beecher would have been the first to have ordered a defense of the treasure to the last. This was sound reasoning . . . as foolish as the reasoning may have seemed!

Feverishly, Giggles took out the precious corner of the map with the figure of the nose drawn upon it . . . and held this parchment scrap up together with the wrinkled circus bill on the back of which he had sketched some crude pencil lines, reproductive of the drawings on the map itself, which was now in the white chieftain's possession.

"Let's have some good light, Bing," said Giggles, excitedly, "I'm going to make another map, drawn right to scale, just as nearly as I can remember it. And when I get it done, by fitting this nose into the corner where it belongs we're going to find out exactly where the treasure's located!"

"Great!" exclaimed Curly, with enthusiasm, as Bing centered the flashlight for Giggles to work by.

"But I haven't any paper or anything to draw the map on!" discovered Giggles, crestfallen.

"Here . . . how about drawing it on the back of my shirt?" asked Curly, peeling his sweater to reveal a white, close-fitting expanse of cloth.

"Fine!" agreed Giggles, taking up the stub of the soft lead pencil so kindly and unwittingly furnished

146

him by the white chieftain. "Sometimes, Curly, I'm almost forced to the conclusion that you've got a brain!"

"Tee, hee, hee!" mimicked Curly. "Same to you!"

CHAPTER XI

THE FICKLE DWARF

THE first thing that Giggles did in his effort to reconstruct the map from memory, was to take the tattered corner of the original (the upper left hand corner, it was), and make a pencil marking around it as he held it flattened against Curly's left shoulder blade.

"Don't you dare move!" Giggles admonished, as Curly held himself rigid while his chum smoothed out the wrinkles in the shirt to get a better drawing surface. "This makes me feel like a Chinese laundry," chuckled Giggles, measuring down Curly's back and pressing in with the pencil point to make a dot.

"Wish I could see what you were doing," lamented Curly.

"Well . . . maybe when I'm done . . . you can take your shirt off," promised Giggles.

"As it is you'll have to stick around pretty close," warned Bing, looking on interestedly. "You're going to be the first walking map in existence."

"You might draw a nice big chocolate bar," suggested Curly. "I knew if you put off eating it till eight o'clock that something would happen to it."

Giggles gave his chum a good-natured poke.

"Dry up, will you?"

"Dry up!" moaned Bing. "I could forget about that chocolate bar if I only had a drink!"

"Waiter, bring this man a glass of ice cold water, will you?" mocked Giggles. But he stopped to purse his own lips.

"Ought to be plenty water here somewhere," said Uncle Eb. "Underground springs."

"That's what we want . . . underground springs," seconded Curly. "Never mind drawing the chocolate bar, Giggles. I've changed my mind. Make it a lake!"

"Say, will you guys keep still? How do you think I can do anything with all that chatter? Besides, it wouldn't be a bad idea for one of you to keep your eyes open for trouble."

"Just as if we haven't got enough trouble without looking for it," remarked Curly. "Excuse me but my foot's gone to sleep. There, that's better. What kind of an easel does my back make anyway? A pretty good one?"

"Oh . . . fair," answered Giggles, pausing a moment to check up on the markings he had made. "I wish you were fatter, though. It's pretty bumpy work most of the time . . . especially when I have to draw a line across your spinal column. Your ribs don't help much either."

Bing and Curly grinned. Uncle Eb, intent on Giggles' work, relaxed enough to wink. Spot gave an impulsive bark.

"How's our friend Tiny Thumb getting along?" asked Giggles, suddenly.

"Gee, I'd almost forgotten about him!" exclaimed Bing, getting up. "I'll see."

He felt his way along until he came to a rock pillar against which the bound dwarf had been placed. He found Tiny Thumb still there, nursing a grouch and inquiring when he was to be released.

"When we get good and ready," Bing announced. "Or when you get ready to talk."

"I'm sore and cramped from lying in one position," complained the dwarf. "Move me around, won't ya?"

"When you get ready to talk," repeated Bing, and returned to report to Giggles.

Work on the map was progressing rapidly and the excitement of all was growing. Uncle Eb, especially, could hardly control his feelings.

"If I'd been able to get the real map it would have been a cinch," apologized Giggles. "All I'd have had to do was to have fitted the nose into the corner of it, where the nose belonged, and then drawn a line straight down from the tip of the nose, a certain number of inches long, and the end of the line would have shown us where the treasure was hidden!"

"What?" ejaculated Bing and Curly together. "How do you know that?"

"I don't know it exactly," hedged Giggles. "I've just got a powerful hunch, that's all. You see there wasn't a place marked on the map—just the underground tracing of the cave with all its passageways. There were some rather queer wordings underneath though, which sort of explained the key. Remember that drawing we found on the back of that door which led into the echo room, and the wording there —'If you hear it—you know'?"

Bing and Curly nodded while Uncle Eb looked on wonderingly.

"Well, on the map this wording was repeated with some more added to it. It said: 'If you hear it— you know you're under the dog's paw'!"

"How funny!" exclaimed Curly. "Dog's paw! What's that have to do with the treasure? What's the dog's paw, anyway?"

"That's what I had to figure out," replied Giggles. "Oh, I've been using my noodle for the last couple of hours. Good thing we didn't get a chance to eat that chocolate bar," he added, wittily. "I can never think after meals!"

"Say!" threatened Curly, "it's a good thing for you that I'm acting as a map or I'd—" He looked back over his shoulder.

"Hold still!" ordered Giggles. "I want to show Bing and Uncle Eb just where echo cave is located."

Giggles had the map fairly well sketched out now. It was a peculiar looking affair, a rather ragged line bounding the drawing which represented the actual size of the original parchment. Giggles had determined the size while examining the genuine article, using his index finger to do it. The parchment paper containing the map was six and a half index fingers long and four index fingers wide. By placing the piece of the map with the figure of the nose on it, into the left hand corner of his drawing, Giggles had been enabled to start his actual tracing of the cave in the same relative position that this tracing appeared in the original. Of course he had had no time to familiarize himself with every nook and cranny of the intricate network of passageways and rooms depicted in the map, but it had not been particularly difficult to sketch what appeared to be the main features in a manner that would permit their setting down again. And Giggles had done an excellent job of it as the wrinkled pencil markings on Curly's somewhat soiled white shirt testified.

"See here," directed Giggles, "the first thing under the sign of the nose is the basement of Uncle Eb's house. That dot there indicates the location of the door leading down into the cave. This crooked line is the first passageway we passed through. Now there's the room of 'The Jumping Lady.' Remember her?"

Bing nodded, eyes gleaming.

"Let me take off my shirt," pleaded Curly. "I want to see!"

"You leave your shirt on!" commanded Giggles. "We'd have a hard time making this map out if it wasn't stretched tight like it is. You can take your shirt off when we get out of here."

"Ow!" groaned Curly. "That means something's going to happen to it. It's going to disappear just like the chocolate bar."

"No it's not!" declared Giggles. "That shirt's a lot more valuable than a little cake of chocolate. We're not going to give *it* up without a fight."

"Gee, that's worse yet!" moaned Curly. "Just where do I come out in this deal, anyway?"

"Wherever you can get out," laughed Giggles, giving Curly a playful shove, only to exclaim, reproachfully, "hold still, won't you?" Then, turning seriously to Bing and Uncle Eb, Giggles continued: "Now see this jog to the left. That takes us into the great big room where we saw the dwarf up on that high ledge. Here's the path that took us around behind that mammoth boulder, and showed us the steps that led us up to the ledge which was named 'The Lookout'."

"How do you know it is?" asked Bing, puzzled.

"Because, once you find where the echo cave is you can locate every place else by it," explained Giggles. "There's a lot I haven't told you yet, and you'll just have to take my word for some things as I go along. Don't forget though that the nose up there in the corner has a great deal to do with it. Important points on the map all fall in a straight line from the end of the nose. That's the key, and that's where the white chieftain, and Redwood, and the colored boy are going to run up against a stump.

Redwood seemed to know something about the nose business but, unless I miss my guess, what he knows won't help much. He didn't seem to know that the missing piece of the map contained the nose or, for that matter, that the nose had anything to do with the map. All he apparently knew was that 'the treasure laid in a straight line from echo cave.' And echo cave is the one thing that the gang have been trying to find."

Uncle Eb shook his head regretfully.

"I tries not to give cave away," he said. "I gets what you tells me fine, about pretendin' to know all about cave . . . and followin' you to where the echo room was, and about shuttin' the door and makin' the sound, and our watchin' a chance to git away . . . but I thinks, if I don't shut the door they don't be no wiser. . . ."

"Good idea," commended Giggles, "but don't you feel bad about putting them on. I failed, too. I tried my darnedest to keep hold of the map, but I couldn't do it without arousing suspicion. That's why I studied the map like I did when I saw how anxious they were to locate the echo room. I thought, if I couldn't get the map, the next best thing would be a good look at it. And say, when we got to where the echo cave was, I was scared stiff for fear all of the gang wouldn't come in. That's why I said for the white chieftain to let you and me go in first. I thought he'd object to that, and he sure did. He brought every one inside, saying we weren't going to get out of his sight. Tee, hee, hee! Wonder what he's saying now?"

There was a low cry from the dwarf man.

"See what he wants," directed Giggles.

"He wants to talk," advised Bing, on coming back. "He says the way he's lying is almost killing him."

"Well, you ask him how we can tell whether he's lying or not if we let him talk," said Giggles, eyes twinkling. Then, as the wondering Bing started to comply, "No, no! I was only kidding. I *thought* he'd come around in a little while. We'll listen to his story in a few minutes. Soon as we finish here . . ."

"Put on a little speed, won't you?" pleaded Curly. "I'm getting tired being a map!"

Again Giggles smoothed out the wrinkles in the back of Curly's shirt and studied the lines he had drawn. He added a few pencil touches at points that he felt had not been brought out clearly enough.

"There were several peculiar wordings on the map," informed Giggles. "Another one was 'What is straight up from the dog's paw?' That's one I haven't been able to figure out yet. Maybe you fellows can help me."

Uncle Eb shook his head helplessly as Bing and Curly gazed at one another.

"My grandfather was crazy," the old hermit reiterated. "Maybe he leads you on wild goose chase. . . ."

"Maybe," grinned Giggles, "but I don't think so.

Looks to me like he was darn clever, and original—figuring out a map like this."

"He was crazy just the same," insisted Uncle Eb, cuffing Spot to make the restless dog lie down beside him.

" 'What is straight up from the dog's paw?' " repeated Giggles. "See this strange formation here, Bing? That should be the dog's paw. It should be if the wording that I told you about a minute ago means anything."

"About 'if you hear it you know you're under the dog's paw?' " asked Bing, reflectively.

"That's it!" said Giggles, putting a finger to his lips in a pondering gesture. "Now what in thunder . . . ?"

"Were there any other wordings that you haven't told us about?" interrupted Curly.

"Why . . . yes . . . but they don't appear to have any connection. There was one that said, 'Don't follow your nose this time.' . . ."

"Hmmm!" said Curly, then he wheeled around excitedly, forgetting the map on his back. "I got it! Say, you're not so smart! It's as plain as the nose on your face."

"What is?"

"What's straight up from the dog's paw!"

"All right, I'll bite."

"The *dog's nose, of course!*"

Giggles looked blank for a moment.

"Yeah," objected Bing, consideringly. "But there

wasn't any mention about which paw—it might have been the dog's tail!"

"Be sensible!" ordered Curly, in genuine excitement. "Can't you see how those wordings fit together? The next wording says, according to Giggles, 'Don't follow your nose this time.' Now what could *that* mean . . . ?"

Giggles and Bing exchange perplexed glances.

"I'll bite again," said Giggles, finally. "My noodle refuses to work any more."

"I guess it *does!*" guyed Curly, eyes dancing, "when you figure out the hard ones and leave the easy ones for me. If I'm right about the dog's nose being straight up from the dog's paw, then that direction about 'not following your nose this time' is just the same as saying . . ."

"Follow the dog's!" cried Giggles and Bing in the same breath. The two chums reached out and shook hands with one another.

"You didn't tell us," kidded Giggles. "We knew it all the time!"

"You fellows make me sick!" exploded Curly, in mock disgust.

"Turn around here now," commanded Giggles, eagerly. "Let's see if we can find anything on this crude map which looks like a dog's nose."

"That ought to be easy," reasoned Bing, "if we've already located the paw."

"Yeah . . . but you couldn't recognize any resemblance to a dog in the map I've drawn," said

Giggles. "We'll just have to locate the nose by inference."

"There's where it *ought* to be!" said Bing, jabbing Curly severely in the back.

"Ouch . . . that's my floating rib!" complained Curly.

"You're right, Bing, there's the spot!" agreed Giggles, giving Curly a second punch.

"Say—cut the comedy!"

Giggles backed away as Curly turned upon him. Uncle Eb actually gave a chuckle of laughter.

"That's just what we're going to do," said Giggles, sobering up. "Cut the comedy. It looks like we've got things pretty well figured out, and we're headed in the right direction—toward the dog's nose. Now to get what we can out of the dwarf, and then—after that treasure!"

"And then—after a drink!" corrected Curly. "My throat's like a piece of sandpaper."

The three chums and Uncle Eb found the dwarf in a much perturbed state of mind. Tiny Thumb was in a rage equal to an average-sized man. Everybody picked on him anyway, just because he was small. He had a stiff neck, a stitch in his back and cramps in both legs. To listen to his tirade one would have thought him the most abused little man in existence.

"You sound a lot different now than you did guarding Uncle Eb when he was chained to that wall," reminded Giggles. "A lot you cared how he might have felt. It wouldn't have bothered you any if they'd burned him with that red hot iron rod. But now, just because we leave you lying here, tied up, for about a half hour, you think you're being tortured. Say, we ought to let you stay right where you are. Little! Humph! That doesn't mean anything in our young lives. You're just as bad as the rest of 'em. And you'd have done just as much damage if you could!"

The dwarf man squirmed and screwed up his face so that all the wrinkles seemed to run together. He was so mad that he looked like the slow motion picture of a firecracker blowing up. But the only difference was, he made no noise. He was so hot he couldn't even sizzle; he was almost melting.

"We're not forgetting that you shot at us, either," added Giggles, "when you were up on that high ledge. That's something else to hold against you."

Tiny Thumb gave a snort at this.

"Huh! You boys think I shot to hit?"

"You came close enough to suit me," answered Bing. "Chipped off the rocks beside us."

"Huh, I'm a crack shot with pistols," said the dwarf. "I didn't have to miss. Think that over." He groaned and twisted. "Let me up, won't ya? Give a fellah a chance!"

"Let him up," consented Giggles.

Curly bent down and untied the rope binding the pygmy man hand and foot. But it was several minutes before Tiny Thumb could move about freely or with any degree of comfort.

"All right, our tying you up didn't injure your voice any, did it?" prodded Giggles, finally. "We've got to be on our way and you promised to talk; there's certain things we want to know."

"Well?" snapped the dwarf, small eyes burning. He was still busy rubbing out kinks in his slender limbs.

"First, what do you know about the treasure?"

"Nothing!"

The reply came with speeding promptness.

"That's certainly not much," said Giggles, glancing at Bing and Curly. Uncle Eb crowded over to peer down at the dwarf, studyingly.

"You're a storyin'!" charged the old hermit, tensely.

"Get away from me!" cried Tiny Thumb in a rage, striking out at his grizzly-faced kidnaper. Giggles pushed Uncle Eb back, gently.

"Never mind him," he ordered. "Pay attention to me. If you don't know anything about the treasure, what *do* you know?"

"I know there's supposed to be a treasure, that's all," answered the dwarf, in his sharp, piping voice. "Redwood knows most. He's been trying for years to get to it. Him and George have been coming here winter an' summer. Before circus starts out an' after circus gets back. This summer George an' Redwood stayed behind—George strained his back

160

rehearsing a lifting act; Redwood had a job at the quarters given to him for letting Big Bill in on the secret."

"Who do you mean by Big Bill?" interrupted Giggles.

"Big Bill, boss of the quarters—'white chief,' Redwood calls him," informed Tiny Thumb.

"Oh . . . !" rejoined the three chums, in chorus.

"And how'd *you* get in on this?" persisted Giggles.

The dwarf shrugged his shoulders as though this question was of little consequence, and that it was also easy of answer.

"I'm sick when the show goes out. An' before I get ready to join the show Big Bill comes to me with a proposition. He and Redwood an' George have been trying to scare that old man there." Tiny Thumb pointed at Uncle Eb. ". . . trying to scare him out of the house, so's they could get in an' find the map what Redwood knew about, an' locate the way into the cave an' find the treasure which Redwood's gran'father helped get!"

"But me an' Spot wouldn't scare, eh?" chuckled Uncle Eb, mightily interested, pulling at the ragged stubble of his whiskers. Spot, spoken to, leaped up and jumped at Tiny Thumb, viciously. Giggles had to cuff the dog away. The dwarf man kicked out at the dog defensively and screwed up his face again which made him look more than a match for the animal.

"Scared?" sniffed Tiny Thumb, scornfully. "Naw,

161

you didn't know enough to be scared, 'cepting when we had you caught and was threatening ya. Then you hollered like a good fellah."

"That was the time to holler," argued Uncle Eb, with a wink at the boys.

"We wouldn't have hurt you none," said the dwarf. "We didn't have it planned to hurt nobody. Just scare 'em, that was all. 'Scare the everlasting daylights out of 'em,' Big Bull used to say, 'but don't do 'em no harm.' Maybe it looked like we was out to cut your throats or shoot you dead . . . but it was all pretend like."

"Of course, if you could have scared any of us to death it would have been all right!" surmised Giggles, dryly.

"Say, I've got a question to ask him!" spoke up Curly, suddenly. "What was the cause of those lights we saw out from the bluff last night?"

"Ha! Ha! Ha!" laughed the dwarf, a shrill cackle which told of his high amusement. "That sort of *got* you, did it?"

"Them 'spirit' lights!" exclaimed Uncle Eb, curiously.

"Yeah, explain *that!*" ordered Giggles.

Tiny Thumb hesitated, cocking his head strangely. A teasing expression came into the wrinkles on his face, as he answered. "Big Bill's an electrician. Figure the rest out for yourselves!"

Then, before the chums could prevent it, Tiny Thumb placed two fingers between his teeth and blew a sharp, high-toned whistle. Giggles, Bing and Curly leaped for the dwarf at once and all but smothered him. The commotion, however, stirred up Spot who commenced an excited barking which Uncle Eb had difficulty in checking. And while the four were endeavoring to restore quiet, a decidedly familiar but nevertheless chilling response came to the shrieking whistle which the dwarf had emitted.

"Ow . . . oooooooh!"

Somehow the cry struck a deeper note of terror this time than ever before. Before, the cry had been shorn of any particular malice—had been used, in fact, largely for experimental purposes in seeking the echo cave. But now the yell had taken on a savage tenor, the unmistakable ring of the war whoop. It gave heart-jumping evidence that the white chieftain, the colored giant and the Indian were indeed on the war path. And it brought to the chums as well as to Uncle Eb, the instant realization that to fall into the hands of this trio again would prove little short of fatal. But Tiny Thumb, who had been uncannily aware of his cronies' approach, now fought with complete abandon, exerting all his small strength in an effort to retard the escape of his captors. Struggle as he would, however, Giggles and Bing bore him along between them, one clutching his head and arms tightly, the other, his feet. And so, led by Curly and Uncle Eb, with Spot bounding on ahead, the dog keeping always on the outer edge of the flashlight rays, Giggles and Bing hurried on, penetrating deeper and deeper into the weird recesses of the great cavern, being driven in the direction which the map indicated as the possible location of the treasure.

CHAPTER XII

ON THE VERGE

"THIS isn't so good!" panted Giggles, when the party paused to rest after a breathless fifteen minutes of flight. "We're headed right but so are they. Talk about not hurting any one. You little double-crosser, you! For two cents I'd just about break you in two!"

The dwarf, bruised from his rough journey, had sufficient spirit to utter a contemptuous grunt of rage.

"Think I'm going to sit by peaceable when I got a chance to get away?" he retorted.

"Did you ever think you might get treated better by us than you would by them if you acted decent?" Giggles flung back.

"Ow . . . ooooh!"

At the cry, Tiny Thumb made a desperate attempt to whistle again but Bing and Curly were too quick for him.

"Gee, they're setting an awful pace!" exclaimed Giggles. "We've got to keep moving!" He laid hold of the dwarf, dividing the burden of the pygmy with Bing as before.

"One more outburst from you," Giggles whispered in Tiny Thumb's ear, "and you're really going to get hurt. This isn't a threat. It's a promise!"

The great and extensive interior yawned beckoningly in all directions as the four plunged their way, holding to as straight a course as they could and not having the slightest idea as to what might open up in front of them. It seemed now as though they were suddenly in the midst of an infinitude of black space, marred by jagged formations of rock, unexpected downward slopes, upward climbs and temporary barriers of wall-like pendants which hung down from an invisible ceiling, or inverted pendants, which jutted up from the floor as though at one time the floor had been the ceiling!

"Say, we're going to get in here so far that we're never going to get out!" voiced Curly, in growing alarm. "I can't go much further without a drink anyway. I don't care what happens!"

"Tee, hee, hee!" giggled Giggles. "Is that all the better camel you are? Don't let up now. That map on your back says we're pretty near to the dog's nose, if there is such a thing!"

"Yeah, but is the dog's nose near a drink?" persisted Curly. "That's the only thing that interests me!"

Bang! Bang!

"Flashlights out!" cried Giggles.

Uncle Eb and Curly, into whose custody the flashlights had been given, clicked them off together.

A glance behind revealed nothing but inky darkness . . . that is, until a red spout of flame burst

166

into another report and a bullet whizzed screamingly overhead.

"That's the white chieftain," informed Giggles. "And that's his little colt that he said was liable to chase us if we didn't be good!"

"They're awfully close!" gasped Bing. "How can they cover ground that way?"

"It's Redwood," guessed Curly.

"Ha! Ha! Ha!" laughed Tiny Thumb. "You're going to get caught again. You're going to get caught!"

"Just you remember not to make a noise," warned Giggles, placing a hand on the nape of the dwarf's neck. "Uncle Eb . . . where's Spot?"

"Bow-wow! Bow-wow-wow!"

"There he is," whispered the old hermit, somewhat tardily, "dead ahead of us, right close to his bark!"

The boys choked nervous snickers. But Uncle Eb saw no humor in the answer he had given. Especially since Spot's outburst had called forth another whistling bullet and an angry shout from the white chieftain.

"Give up? You can't get away from us! Give up an' we'll talk thin's over. We ain't goin' to hurt you if you acts sensible!"

"Oh, no!" murmured Giggles. "You wouldn't do a thing to us this time! Not a thing!"

Of a sudden a flashlight beamed from behind, the flashlight which had belonged to Bing. The rays were not quite strong enough to reach the little party up ahead but the light did reveal how alarmingly close the pursuers actually were. Apparently the white chieftain had deemed it wise to do away with the torch which Redwood had carried and to rely entirely upon the pocket flash. As the beam was swung searchingly about the cavernous interior, Uncle Eb led the boys forward single file, feeling his way through the pitch blackness and trying desperately to put more distance between the furthermost reach of the flashlight and themselves. So long as they could keep out of sight they were reasonably safe.

But Spot! Crazy dog that he was—meaning well, yet causing more trouble than he had caused good! And now Spot proceeded to notify the pursuing trio of the exact whereabouts of the escaping quartet by a series of frantic yelpings. Uncle Eb, first to get to Spot, grabbed at his dog in an effort to silence the animal. Spot, however, aided by the darkness, slipped from all clutches and continued a piteous howling, there seeming to be frenzied terror in the dog's bark.

"Go on!" urged Giggles. "Never mind trying to catch Spot. They'll be up on us any minute. Keep going!"

The boys, now abreast of one another, Giggles and Bing each grasping the dwarf by an arm and dragging him between them, started on. This movement transformed Spot's whines into snaps and snarls.

Leaping in front of them, Uncle Eb's dog tried his best to prevent the taking of another step. Angered, Giggles cried out to whoever might be able to lay hands on Spot.

"Kill him! Do anything! The dog's gone mad. Get him out of the way!"

Bang! Bang!

"Use your flashlights!" Giggles ordered. "We've got to take a chance. Keep them down and right in front of you so they won't throw much light. . . ."

Uncle Eb and Curly did as directed. With the light came hushed exclamations of surprise and bewilderment. Although the lights were pointed toward what should have been the floor of the cavern, their beams failed to reflect anything but inky darkness. For a moment the boys stood, rubbing their eyes. The rays were apparently as strong as ever, and why they revealed not so much as an outline just a few feet ahead was indeed astounding. Uncle Eb, puzzled, took a step ahead, only to be pounced upon by Spot, the dog sinking his teeth in a tattered trouser knee and hanging on despite several sharp cuffings.

"Something's wrong!" cried Curly. "We can't see any cave any more. We can't see anything ahead of us! Gee . . . !"

"Look out!" screamed Giggles, releasing his hold on the dwarf to leap toward Uncle Eb.

The old hermit, in shaking off Spot, had taken another step forward and dropped from sight . . . all save his fingers which had clawed for a hold and caught on a small rock formation. This rocky ledge seemed poised on the edge of darkness and it was toward the clawing fingers that Giggles lunged. Loose stones, dislodged in Uncle Eb's drop, could now be heard descending what appeared to be a precipitous decline and the flashlight, which Uncle Eb had let fall, was visible to Giggles as it flashed—end over end—down, down, down, occasionally striking some projection a glancing blow, bouncing off with a metallic sound, and continuing on and on, down . . . down . . . until it was heard to strike far below—a faint splashing sound echoing up.

"Help, quick!" gasped Giggles, catching Uncle Eb's slipping fingers and gaining a hold on the old hermit's wrist. Spot leaped in and tried to aid, dog fashion, only getting in the way as he sought to grip his master's sleeve. Bing and Curly grasped Giggles, each by a leg, as their chum prostrated himself to keep the clutch on Uncle Eb who had now lost his hold on the rocks and was dangling, feet down, over the terrifying abyss. Giggles kept both hands tightly clamped about the hermit's right wrist and strained every muscle to prevent his being drawn over the edge himself.

It was an effort made in complete darkness for Curly had been forced to abandon his flashlight in laying hold of Giggles. And, as Bing and Curly braced to afford an anchor for Giggles in the pull to remove Uncle Eb from his precarious position, they were set upon from behind by a tiny form which assailed them with great fury. The dwarf! Attacking now when his small force would be magnified many times because of the tremendous disadvantage they were under.

Bing sank to his knees as Tiny Thumb threw his body against him. But Bing dared not release his hold on Giggles to fight back. Curly was next assaulted, the dwarf encircling Curly's legs with his short arms and exerting such pressure that Curly fell heavily to the floor of the cavern.

The downward pull of Uncle Eb who had reached up with his other hand to seize Giggles' wrist in a deathlike grip, now began to drag all three chums toward the edge and a black oblivion beyond.

"What's the matter with you fellows?" cried Giggles, despairingly. "Pull! Don't push! We're going over!"

"It's the dwarf!" gasped Bing. "He's fighting us, we're doing all we . . . !"

"Bow-wow-wow! Bow-wow-wow!"

"Sic 'em, Spot!" pleaded Giggles. "Sic 'em!"

"Big Bill! This way! Redwood! George!" screamed Tiny Thumb. "I got 'em! They're goners! Hurry!"

"Coming!" bellowed a voice some distance away, while a light moved unevenly up and down.

"Sic 'em, Spot! Sic 'em!" cried Bing and Curly, trying desperately to regain their feet only to be pushed down by the pygmy man who took great care to keep behind them as they slipped slowly . . . resistingly . . . toward the great, black opening in the floor of the cavern. Spot whined, not seeming to realize what was wanted of him and crawled up, in the darkness, to lick at the boys' faces. In doing so he bumped against the dwarf man, and Tiny Thumb made one mistake, he kicked out in the darkness, afraid of Spot's friendly relations since the dog had been called upon for aid, the kick landing on Spot's jaw. Just then, Uncle Eb, aware of the struggle that was going on in his behalf, gasped out:

"Spot! Go get 'em! Eat 'em up!"

And, from that moment on, Spot—ordinarily the most peaceful of animals—became a raging little dynamo. His first murderous leap in the darkness bowled the dwarf over, and Tiny Thumb was engaged for the next few minutes in trying to keep his Adam's apple from being chewed to pieces.

"Sic 'em, Spot! That's the dog!" encouraged Bing and Curly as they braced against the rock ledge and set themselves for the pull which would determine whether they had strength enough left to save Uncle Eb. It is surprising how the dead weight of one individual can exert such a stupendous pull upon others when hanging straight down and the pull is from above. It seemed, in the next few seconds, as though the two chums must release their holds upon Giggles and let him plunge to a probable death along with Uncle Eb, for Giggles, despite the torture he was experiencing, would never have relinquished his grip voluntarily. Giggles was now head down, his body over the precipice to the waist. A part of the rock ledge gave way, sending a shower of fragments hurtling past Giggles' face and just missing Uncle Eb's head. Curly groped frantically for a new footing.

"You, you can't make it, boys!" faltered Uncle Eb. "Never mind. Let me drop! I don't want to be takin' you with me! It's all right. . . ."

"Hold on!" gasped Giggles. "Oh, if we only had a light—if we could see what we were doing!"

Struggling grimly at the very brink, Curly and Bing gave a mighty tug and felt the body of Giggles scrape back over the edge.

"Once more!" cried Curly, encouraged.

Again the two chums pulled together, knowing that—should this effort fail—they would be doomed. Their strength was soon to give out.

"That's the stuff!" urged Giggles. "Keep it up! My arms! They feel like their coming out of their sockets. Keep it up!"

"Let me go!" pleaded Uncle Eb. "I'm too heavy . . . I'll . . . !"

"Help! Help! Call this dog off . . . call this dog off!" begged the dwarf, now having all he could do to combat Spot in the darkness.

Another desperate heave and Giggles regained his position atop the ledge with Unble Eb still below . . . just too low to prevent his being of any help to himself. The strain was telling on Curly especially.

"I—I've just got to let go for a second," he groaned. "Have you got a good hold, Bing? How're you fixed, Giggles?"

"Make it snappy!" was Giggles only comment.

"Find that flashlight!" cried Bing. "I was stepping on it a minute ago . . . I'll hang till . . . !"

Curly released his grip on Giggles, an involuntary sigh of relief escaping his lips at the removing of strain from a cramped arm. He groped wildly about on the rock ledge.

"I—I can't find it!" he gasped. "Hadn't I better . . . ?"

"Keep hunting! It can't be very far away! We've got to have it!"

"Here! Here!" screamed the dwarf. "Here's the flashlight! Call off that dog!"

"Turn the light on!" ordered Curly. "Turn it on if you've got it!"

A seeming eternity of suspense, during which time the chums were not at all sure but what the fickle Tiny Thumb was spoofing. Then . . .

"There!"

The light clicked on, showing Spot snapping savagely at the dwarf man who lay flat on his back some feet away from the brink, kicking savagely.

"Spot!" yelled Curly, making a leap for Uncle Eb's dog. "Here, boy!"

Things happened in startlingly quick fashion from that moment on. The chums had completely forgotten any peril outside their own. It mattered not, now, how near or how far the white chieftain and his two rough cohorts were. All that mattered was the release from their present predicament. Curly sent Spot sprawling to one side as he reached out and tore the flashlight from the dwarf's stunted fingers. Whirling its rays toward the edge of the precipice and the wall of impenetrable darkness, he lunged back, leaning over the ledge to grasp at Uncle Eb's body. He caught the old hermit under an arm pit and, with the light enabling the chums to see what they were doing, Uncle Eb was slowly pulled to the top and finally dragged back from the shadowy depths, exhausted. Every one was exhausted, in fact, even the dwarf man who sat, panting for breath, eyes bulging, looking anxiously over his shoulder in quest of the strange trio who were on their way to rescue him.

"Gee!" breathed Giggles, "that's the narrowest escape yet!" He turned upon Tiny Thumb. "You yellow little runt, you! You thought you'd get rid of us all, didn't you? We don't show you any mercy from now on!"

"Ow . . . oooooh!"

"Where are you?" boomed the voice of the white chieftain.

The dwarf put fingers to his lips but Bing was too quick for him. A back-handed slap across the mouth sent the pygmy man flat upon his back while Curly, taking no chances, grabbed Spot and clamped a hand over the dog's jaws.

175

"Say, that's great!" whispered Giggles. "They've run into a wall or something, and they're lost, for the time being—that gives us a chance to get away!"

"I've got to have a drink!" insisted Curly. "My throat is raw!"

"Cheer up, I'll bet it rains to-morrow!"

"No kidding, I . . . !"

"How are you, Uncle Eb?" Giggles inquired, paying no heed to Curly. "Feel like you could travel a little further. . . . ?"

The old hermit raised himself painfully and rubbed his wrists. Then nodded his head and crawled shakily to his feet.

"Which way?" he asked.

"Right along the edge of this pit, here," directed Giggles, in a low voice. "Curly, let Uncle Eb take care of Spot. You go ahead with the flash and don't let out any more light than you absolutely have to. Bing and I will take care of Tiny Thumb. Bing . . . tear off a piece of your shirt. We're going to gag this little fellow whether he likes it or not!"

CHAPTER XIII

ENTOMBED!

IT was the work of a minute to tie a band about the dwarf's mouth so securely that there was no possibility of his making a further outcry. Tiny Thumb was wise enough to know now that the boys would brook no further treacherous move on his part and his meek submission to their treatment of him sharply contrasted his attitude when he felt that he had held the upper hand. The dwarf voluntarily accompanied the boys as they set out, stealthily, making their way with great care to avoid noise or the danger of again stumbling too close to that bottomless void which had almost swallowed them up.

"Not wishing the white chieftain any bad luck at all," whispered Giggles, "but what if he'd walk off this precipice into nothingness? Oh, boy!"

"No chance," mourned Bing. "Bad eggs usually get all the good breaks!"

Progress was continued without any untoward incident until the party had left the mysterious and terrifying chasm behind, the cavern narrowing down and a peculiar pointed bluff coming into view.

"Hello, what's this?" demanded Curly. "Can I give it a real flash?"

Giggles stared cautiously into the awesome darkness behind. They had heard cries from time to time but the sounds had dropped further and further back, indicating that the boys and Uncle Eb were gaining on their pursuers.

"All right," decided Giggles. "Let out the light, and let's see if we can figure out where we are!"

Curly did as directed and the party gazed about for breathless seconds, while each one searched for tell-tale signs or some sight which might offer a suggestion.

"Look—there's three passageways over there," pointed out Bing. "Right side by side. Wonder where they lead to?"

"I still haven't got a drink," reminded Curly.

"Honest, you're fussier than an old woman!" chided Giggles. "Isn't it damp enough down here for you? Why don't you lick some of the moisture off these stones?"

"I'm going to pretty soon," said Curly. "Watch me!"

"Come over here while we take a good look at this big cliff-like rock with the ridge running down through the center, will you?"

Curly obliged, grumblingly. He played the light from the flashlight up and down the mountain of stone and at the irregular ceiling overhead. The dwarf hobbled over, still gagged, and peered about with his tiny eyes looking like two black shoe buttons. Of a sudden the dwarf bent over and gesticulated wildly, pointing at the base of the rock.

"By Jingo!" exclaimed Giggles, excitedly. "He sees something, a lettering!"

The boys and Uncle Eb went down on their knees, the dwarf man brushing away with his hands and twisting up his mouth to puff at particles of dirt which persisted in clinging to the half-covered wording. At length the entire lettering was revealed and when it was, the boys gasped.

DON'T FOLLOW YOUR NOSE THIS TIME

"Whoopee!" cried Curly, exultingly. "So you'd like to know where we are, would you, Mr. Giggles Hungerford? Well, we're right smack up against the dog's nose. And it's just as I figured out before . . . all we got to do is to follow . . ."

". . . the dog's nose!" interrupted Giggles, eyes gleaming. "Yes, sir . . . I'm right with you, Mr. Curly Lamb, right with you!"

"And we're right near the treasure!" added Bing. "If this isn't blundering our way along, I'll . . . I'll . . . well, I'll take a good, big drink of water!"

"Ow . . . !" groaned Curly. "Just as I was beginning to forget about it!"

Uncle Eb placed gnarled hands on the great ridge which ran up the middle of the rock.

"S'pose this is the nose you boys is talkin' about?" he asked, blinkingly. Spot approached the ridge and sniffed at it suspiciously.

"Tee, hee, hee!" giggled Giggles. "Spot says it

179

doesn't look like any dog's nose he ever saw before!"

"Have to hand it to Tiny Thumb for uncovering that wording," said Bing. "We might never have noticed it. . . ."

The dwarf pinched Curly's leg to command attention, motioning at the gag in his mouth and pointing to the map Giggles had drawn on the back of Curly's shirt. By the gestures it was evident that Tiny Thumb wished to impart some information.

"Shall we take the gag out?" asked Bing.

"Go ahead," consented Giggles. "He's tried his best to show us that he's reformed lately. Let's put him on probation."

As soon as the dwarf had his mouth rid of the cloth gag, he spat violently several times and cleared his throat before attempting to talk.

"Bend over, you!" he said, in a voice which was exceedingly weak.

"Talking to me?" asked Curly.

The dwarf nodded. Curly dropped down on his knees obediently, with a wondering glance at Giggles who took the flashlight from him to center its beams on Curly's back.

Standing on tiptoe, Tiny Thumb squinted at Giggles' crudely penciled map, pointing a finger at the spot they had now reached.

"Here's where Redwood wanted to get!" he piped.

Giggles raised his brows in surprise.

"Is it? How do you know? Why?"

Tiny Thumb looked up, a bit confused at the battery of questions.

"Redwood said that Blue Eagle, his grandfather, said to White Pigeon, his father, the last time he was home that . . ."

"For the love of Pete!" ejaculated Curly, turning his head, "what's this—a house that Jack built? Get down to the core of the apple and cut out the peelings!"

". . . that after you found echo cave the treasure lay in a straight line," resumed the dwarf, glowering at Curly. "But Redwood's all mixed up. All echo cave does is to show you where you are so's you can find other places. Don't the map say, 'If you hear it you know you're under the dog's paw'?"

"Say, you're not so dumb, are you?" complimented Giggles.

Tiny Thumb actually let loose enough wrinkles in his face to smile at that. His little shoe button size eyes glowed with genuine interest.

"Me? Brother, I knows more about that map than any of them! I studied it, I did. And when that bird there says we're right smack up against the dog's nose, the whole thing opens up to me just like a picture!"

"What—the nose?" asked Bing, innocently.

"No, the map!" answered the dwarf, with a flare of indignation. "And this here place is where the treasure lies in a straight line from . . . not echo cave!"

The chums glanced at one another consideringly.

"Hmmm! I'm not so sure of that," remarked Giggles, finally. "But thanks for your ideas anyway." Then, in a mimicking voice he imitated the white chieftain. "That's bein' sensible. As long as you acts sensible, I acts sensible. So if you don't want to get hurt, all you got to do is to keep on actin' sensible!"

"Oh, be yourself!" retorted the dwarf in disgust, and the chums laughed. But they could tell that his vicious attitude toward them had changed. He seemed to have reconciled himself to his position and was apparently eager to help all he could. Even so, they would have to watch him closely. His slyness before had almost cost them their lives. This sudden change in attitude might be the cleverest of poses effected toward the accomplishment of a dire purpose!

"It ought to be easy for us to follow the dog's nose," speculated Giggles, "with the nose so unmistakably plain. Wait a minute," as Curly started to rise, "I want to see here which passageway the nose leads to, according to the map. . . ."

Giggles smoothed out the creases in Curly's shirt.

"I don't understand yet how you came to wear a white shirt camping," he remarked. "Unless it was just so I could draw a map on it!"

"I hate to tell you," confessed Curly, "but mother's to blame for it. She said I'd been wearing the shirt and that it was dirty but not too dirty. Her orders were to keep on wearing it till I'd gotten it good and dirty. But she didn't say anything about your drawing pictures all over it!"

"Ah, wait till she sees it. She'll probably never wash it again!" kidded Giggles.

"And that's the truth!" seconded Curly.

"Too bad I didn't have water colors to use," lamented Giggles.

"If you had I'd have drunk 'em all up!"

"Ouch!" exclaimed Bing. "There he goes again!"

"He's got water on the brain," diagnosed Giggles.

"But none in my stomach," prompted Curly. "Are you through tickling my back?"

"Just about. If my drawing's anywhere near accurate we take the middle passageway. Now let's start in that 'straight line' that Redwood said his grandfather, Blue Eagle, said was the way to find the treasure . . . and see if this dog's nose takes us to the middle one of the three passageways over there. They're so close together that we'll have to be careful we don't pick the wrong one!"

Uncle Eb was the first to pace off the distance from the ridge that his grandfather, Ebenezer Beecher, had dubbed "the dog's nose," to the passageway directly across. The intervening space was marred by rough ground and slight detours were necessary to get around rock mounds so that the following of any nose was uncommonly difficult. But Uncle Eb brought up at the mouth of the middle passageway, as Giggles had figured, and all other members of the party did likewise.

"Hurrah!" cried Bing. "We're almost there!"

"Where?" demanded Giggles.

"Where we're going!"

"Oh," said Giggles, softly, "that's different. I thought you'd seen the treasure already. Say—do you fellows realize that this one flashlight is the only light we've got now? And is it my imagination, or is this light actually beginning to grow dim?"

"Gee!" exclaimed Curly, soberly. "We haven't got so much as a match. We'll never get out of here without a light. Think of how far we've come!"

"Maybe it isn't as far as it seems," rejoined Giggles, optimistically. "We've covered the same ground several times."

"Yes . . . but it's far enough," declared Bing. "The thing for us to have done was to have turned back when we got away . . . instead of trying to find the treasure. We had a chance to get away then . . . and get help . . . but now we're blocked in . . . the white chieftain and his two pals are between us and the entrance to the cave. We haven't got a thing to defend ourselves with. We're cold— I am, anyway. And hungry, not to mention . . ."

"Thirsty!" exploded Curly.

"Say, what *is* this, a mutiny?" demanded Giggles. "You don't hear me kicking, do you? Or Uncle Eb? Or . . . or Spot!"

"Why don't you count me in?" asked Tiny Thumb, unexpectedly. "I ain't meaning to go against you no

184

more. Honest. Here's a box of matches to prove it!"

The dwarf produced a small metal box as the chums stared. He handed it over to Giggles who took it and gave it a quick, recognizing glance.

"Thanks," he said, "I sure appreciate having my own things returned to me! Can you beat that, he gives me back the matchbox that Big Bill took from me when he frisked us back in the echo cave!"

The dwarf grinned broadly.

"Got anything else of ours?"

Tiny Thumb shook his head.

"Ain't you glad I had that?"

Giggles laughed. "Well, you got me there. I must admit, I *am!* All right, fellows, come on! It's only ten A.M. Think of it! That's not bad. We're not actually suffering from anything yet. The idea of any one even suggesting thirst. Why I knew a guy once who went fifteen days without a drop of water."

"Go on!"

"Yeah . . . he was on a milk diet!"

How could Bing or Curly long remain self-sympathetic under the influence of such a character as Giggles? Despite all they had gone through he was still forever chasing the blues. Perhaps they *had* erred in not abandoning all efforts to locate the treasure that was supposed to be hidden somewhere. Perhaps they *had* taken a foolhardy chance in pushing on after their escape from the white chieftain, the colored giant and the Indian. Perhaps the sensible thing to have done, since so much emphasis had been placed upon "being sensible," was the direct opposite of what they had done. There was no questioning but that they were still in a most hazardous position any way that the situation could be considered. And while they were apparently enticingly near to a solution of the whole baffling mystery—at least concerning the location of the treasure—they were, at the same time, probably facing the most dangerous experience in their whole underground adventure. Just how dangerous none of the chums could foresee. And though they may have anticipated further hardship, their natural love for penetrating into the farthermost reaches of this great unknown, which had opened up to them since their discovery of the cave, had sufficiently dulled their personal fears to make perseverence desired above all things.

It was this indomitable spirit then, which carried the boys down this forbidding middle passageway until the party came to a halt facing a dark veined wall of rock dead ahead and a passageway splitting two ways, like the top of a letter T.

And, traced in bold white letters, on the wall in front of them, was the wording:

WHICHEVER WAY YOU TURN IS DEATH—
TAKE YOUR CHOICE!

E. B.

"Your grandfather had a funny streak in him," observed Giggles, dryly, with a glance at Uncle Eb.

"There's nothin' funny in that!" shuddered the old hermit, nervously. "It's just like he talked. And he meant what he said, he did! I don't believe we better go no further, boys! Uncle Eb doesn't want you to come to no harm through him."

"Tee, hee, hee!" giggled Giggles. "Now surely you don't mean that, Uncle Eb. After your telling us what a brave man you were . . . and what a brave dog Spot was. Don't you remember?"

Uncle Eb scratched a grizzled chin, uncertainly.

"Yee——es! But that there was above ground. You didn't hear me say nothin' elaborate below ground, did you?"

"How about it, Spot?" asked Giggles, reaching down to pat Uncle Eb's dog on the head. "You going back on your word, too?"

"Bow-wow-wow!"

"There . . . did you hear that? He said, 'I should say not!' Your grandfather can't hurt you now. He can't hurt us either. You certainly know that!"

"Well, if he can't, he can make you feel darned uncomfortable," compromised Uncle Eb. "And I ain't so sure."

"There she goes!"

"The light's out!"

"Now we're in for it!"

"What did I tell you . . . ? It's my grand-father's doin's!"

"Bow-wow-wow!"

"Gee, it's dark!"

"Where's that matchbox I gave you?"

"Don't get excited!" said Giggles in a voice which he tried hard to steady. "We're all right. We'll find a stick somewhere and make a fire brand."

"Yeah, sticks are so plentiful down here!"

Gradually the eyes of all became accustomed to the blackness—as accustomed as human eyes can become. And it was Uncle Eb, whose eyes had long been trained at seeing in the dark, who made the important discovery.

"Say, boys . . . isn't that a wee shaft of light off down that right passageway?"

The chums strained their eyes in a searching stare.

"Sure looks like it," admitted Curly. "Looks almost like daylight!"

"Not quite that good," corrected Giggles. "But I do see what Uncle Eb means. Come on. You game to go with me and see what it is?"

"Might as well as stand here."

"All right. Get bunched close together and get a hold of hands. I'm only going to strike a match as I have to. And, Uncle Eb, I'm going to ask you to lead the way!"

It was, in this manner, that the little caravan on foot started out, creeping along a narrow passageway. Hearts leaped with hope as the strand of light, observed from afar, broadened slowly into a dull, gray glow. And gradually it could be perceived that the party was approaching a shallow, queer-looking white-walled room.

Giggles spent six precious matches on the journey to the room but, once arrived, a half-light which seemed to come from another cavern still ahead, provided enough illumination for the immediate surroundings to be discerned unaided.

And such a sight as the boys witnessed when their eyes had become familiar with the objects before them!

Wooden and metal chests, thrown open . . . partially filled with trinkets of silver and gold and brass and bronze. Early relics of settler days; unique pieces of pottery; marvelous weavings; all manner of household contrivances; heavy pieces of silverware; an indescribable assortment of odds and ends, all of recognizable value because of age and quality. The scene was one of wildest disorder. It appeared as though this wealth had been transported to the room with great care, only to have been dumped or thrown about with reckless abandon, once the depositing room had been reached. Awestruck, the boys and Uncle Eb and Tiny Thumb climbed in and about the maze of chests and treasure, sorting it over and examining it. Each was too impressed to say anything. In fact, it was Tiny Thumb who first gave utterance and then his outcry concerned something foreign to that which was engaging the attention of all.

"Boys! Did you see that flash? Where'd that come from?"

Giggles, Bing and Curly consulted one another. They had been so thoroughly engrossed. No, they had seen nothing. What had the flash looked like? From where had it seemed to come? The boys were disposed to regard Tiny Thumb with new suspicion. What was he up to now?

"Did you see anything, Uncle Eb?" inquired Giggles.

The old hermit shook his head, gazing about uneasily.

"All right!" snapped the dwarf, sullenly. "Then I'm mistaken. But don't say I double-crossed you fellahs again if Big Bill and George and Redwood bust in on ya!"

The three chums started and looked toward the entrance, anxiously. Giggles crept over to investigate. The eery light from the room carried out into the passageway for thirty or more paces. Not a sound or sight of anything. Giggles turned back. It was so easy for one's imagination to picture sounds and sights that didn't happen. Especially in such a weird place as this.

"I think you must have been mistaken," he said to Tiny Thumb. "But just the same, you come away from the entrance to this room. Get over there on the farther side where we can watch you!"

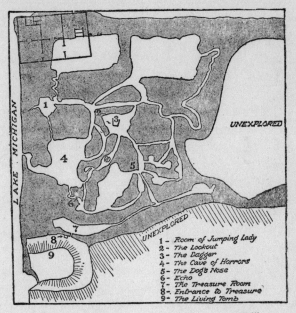

1 – Room of Jumping Lady
2 – The Lookout
3 – The Dagger
4 – The Cave of Horrors
5 – The Dog's Nose
6 – Echo
7 – The Treasure Room
8 – Entrance to Treasure
9 – The Living Tomb

"FIGURE THIS OUT—THE TREASURE IS THINE!"

[page 191]

The dwarf obeyed with a shrug of his tiny shoulders. And it was, while on his way to the point directed, that he called attention to some writing on the wall, black lettering against a white background.

NINE TIMES THE NOSE——LAID A STRAIGHT LINE
FIGURE THIS OUT——THE TREASURE IS THINE!

Dumbly, the three chums and Uncle Eb crowded up to read the above and to scratch their heads, individually and collectively.

"But—but—this *is* the treasure!" faltered Curly.

"Not according to that poetry," deduced Giggles. "This is just . . . just . . . well, just the first smell! Here, turn around, that crazy verse gives me an idea!"

Curly turned his back and Giggles strained his eyes to make out the tracings of the map on the shirt. He finally tossed the matchbox to Bing, asking his chum to strike a light while he did some figuring.

"Let's see, here's the original drawing of the nose," said Giggles, taking the scrap of the genuine map from his pocket. "Nine times this!" He did some measuring of the length of the nose which chanced to be the length of his pencil with a fraction of an inch to spare. Fitting the nose into its accustomed place—the left hand upper corner of the map—Giggles made a dot at the tip end of the nose and then started, laboriously, to measure off a line straight from this tip, leading down across the rather intricate markings of the map, until he had multiplied the length of the original nose nine times!

"There . . . now . . . where are we?" asked Giggles. "Another match, please, Bing! This darn thing is getting exciting!"

A dot made at the end of the measurement revealed a location closely approximating the spot where they actually were.

"Hmmm!" studied Giggles, gazing about. "The real treasure's within a stone's throw of us. And the chances are it's hidden else old Ebenezer Beecher would never have given us this cue to find it!"

"Are you sure you know what you're talking about?" asked Bing, dubiously.

"Absolutely!" answered Giggles. "Look! This line from the end of the nose runs straight down, directly through echo cave. Where we've been confused is the following a straight line to get here when the straight line business referred mostly to the map." Giggles turned to Tiny Thumb who was trying his best to comprehend it all. "You and Redwood were beating all around the bush but neither of you were in it. E.B. intended for whoever might try to find the treasure to follow their noses and the dog's nose to get here, but the key to the place where the treasure was secreted was contained entirely in the map. Don't you see how perfectly everything works out?"

The dwarf shook his head helplessly.

"I don't know so much about that map as I thought I did," he said.

"Here, let's go back here, in the direction that this dot indicates, and prove it out," suggested Giggles, pushing further into the gloomy room, toward the spot where the light seemed to enter. Another passageway presented itself, and—through it—Giggles thought he could detect a low, pounding sound. Spot leaped on ahead with a joyous bark.

"What's that fool dog see?" wondered Uncle Eb.

"It's the *lake!*" cried Giggles, a moment later.

"Water!" yelled Curly, "good old H_2O! And it's lots lighter in here, too! Oh, boy, shall I dive in?"

"Wait a minute. Don't go off your noodle!" warned Giggles. "Take it easy. Look around here a bit before you do anything rash. Can you imagine such a place as this? A regular underground pool! Look down in that water, she's deep! And see that ledge that the water comes up under? I'll bet we're right next to the outside edge of the bluff . . . the lake's just on the other side of that ledge. But say, that ledge goes down under water about twenty feet! Wonder how thick the ledge is?"

Giggles' speculations were lost upon the party as the first thought of every one else was to get a drink at all costs. Tiny Thumb had considerable difficulty in stooping over far enough to reach the water so Giggles, grabbing him by the ankles, held him— head down—while the dwarf scooped up handfuls of water and gulped eagerly. Then Giggles himself indulged in a long draught which aroused instant protest from Curly.

"Hey—there! I thought you weren't thirsty!"

Giggles raised his head, mouth dripping.

"I'm not . . . but if I don't get in a good drink now you'll have the whole lake!"

Their thirst satisfied, the boys and Uncle Eb began an exploration of the large, semi-circular room. A heavy wooden beam over the entrance through which they had come, arrested their attention. The beam seemed to be wedged in between two rocks as if for a purpose.

"Wonder what that was put there for?" questioned Curly.

"Give me a hoist. . . . I'm going to climb up on it and see if I can find out," said Giggles.

Bing and Curly lent their shoulders and Giggles soon swung up, astraddle the beam.

"Hello! There's a message carved on the top side of this," informed Giggles. "But I'll have to have some matches to make it out. Pass 'em up, will you, Bing?"

As Bing started to do so there came a sudden flash of light through the passageway and a murderously familiar cry.

"Ow . . . oooooh!"

"What did I tell you?" screamed the dwarf. "Mistaken, was I?"

But before the charging Redwood, followed by the colored giant and the white chieftain, could reach

the interior of the furthermost room in the cave
. . . an even more startling thing happened . . .

The beam, on which Giggles was sitting, gave
way with a rocking crash, being followed by a rum-
bling detonation as seeming tons of dirt and boulders
came thundering down to seal up the entrance as
thoroughly as though the party had been locked inside a vault!

For palpitating seconds there was too much dust
and confusion for any one of the five to determine
how the others had fared.

Giggles, feeling the beam tremble, had leaped
with a cry of warning and had just cleared the
débris. His cry had probably saved the others also,
though all bore minor bruises from flying stones or
rolling rocks. Truly the narrowest of escapes!

And, certainly diabolical in its coincidence, the
beam had struck upright, being supported by the
earthen mass about it . . . the top side turned
toward the boys so that the wording, carved in the
wood, was easily decipherable.

HA! HA! HA! NOW YOU DID IT, DIDN'T YOU?

E. B.

Could the boys or Uncle Eb have heard the actual
ghostly voice of old Ebenezer Beecher they could
not have been more paralyzed by the significance of
these carved words. Crafty old pirate! How his
highly stimulated mind had exerted itself to provide

this last, fiendish trap for whosoever might dare his manufactured horrors and his threats in the searching out of the treasure he had taken such strenuous pains to hoard!

"Tee, hee, hee!" was Giggles' answer to the carving. "We sure did do it, E.B. Or rather, *I* did! Golly, I wonder what happened to the white chieftain and the colored giant and that Indian? Do you fellows suppose they were crushed?"

There was no way of telling; the boys could only conjecture. Dazedly they looked around, being conscious of waves pounding sluggishly against the other side of the rock ledge which projected down into the water. The hollow boom! . . . boom! . . . began to get on their nerves. They could tell by the light which struggled in from outside through the water that they were near the outside world . . . and yet . . . so far! Gradually the terrorizing realization of their position dawned upon them and they stared at each other wide-eyed. But it was Uncle Eb who voiced the gnawing fear which had crept into every heart.

"I was afeared of somethin' like this! I was afeared of it! No human bein's ever beat my grandfather yet. And we ain't either. My glory, boys, do ye reckon what's took place? *We're entombed!*"

CHAPTER XIV

THE DEATH CHANCE

ENTOMBED! The word seemed to echo against the inner wall of the bluff and come hurtling back with increased force, increased meaning. Entombed! Bottled up underground! Buried beneath tons upon tons of mighty rock hanging overhead! Tortured by the soft swish of water seeping under the ledge—a ledge which now became a cruel barrier—a monster laughing at all thoughts of escape!

It was useless to place any hope upon getting out the way they had come in. And no other possible exit could be found. It was rock . . . rock . . . rock . . . everywhere! Frenziedly the chums covered every foot of the cave along the rough wall, beating the unresponsive stone with their fists, hoping—yes, praying—that some spot would give up a hollow sound and would reveal a secret passageway to lead them out of their extreme dilemma. But no such good fortune was theirs. At length, weary and grave-faced, they sat down near the pool to talk things over.

"It's twelve o'clock noon," announced Giggles. "To-day's Tuesday, and none of our folks will even suspect anything wrong until late Saturday, if then.

We told them that we might stay over until next Monday."

"And nobody'd ever miss me!" lamented Uncle Eb. " 'ceptin' Spot," he added, as his faithful dog came up to lick his hand. "What do ye think of this fix we're in anyhow, partner?"

"Bow wow!"

"As much as that? Well, well!"

"One good thing, we've got plenty of water," said Curly.

"Yes, we can get along without chocolate bars a lot longer than we can without aqua," declared Giggles.

"But that isn't getting us out of here," objected Bing. "And it's not at all certain that our folks or anybody would ever find where we are if they did miss us!"

"They'd probably go to the house on the bluff, and run on to the cave," reasoned Giggles.

"Yeah, they'd probably do that," agreed Bing. "That would be simple. The hard part would be from then on."

"And in the meantime we'd be dying a slow death," meditated Curly. "Gee, doesn't it give you an awful feeling to be cooped up in this place? It wasn't so bad to be lost because you sort of knew that it would just be a matter of time before you could stumble on the way out. But now there's no way out—for us! And Saturday a million years away!"

"Maybe Big Bill or Redwood or George . . . they get scared and tell somebody," spoke up the dwarf, hopefully.

"Not likely," discouraged Giggles. "If they survived they're probably thanking their lucky stars at what happened to us. And if they're scared it's the other way around. They're so scared that they aren't ever going to say a thing. They're just going to get what they can and beat it!"

Tiny Thumb eyed Giggles shrewdly, and grinned.

"You knows 'em pretty well, don't you?" he asked.

"You bet!" snapped Giggles. "Isn't that what you'd have done if you'd still been with them?"

"Say, listen," said the dwarf, confidentially. "I'll tell you boys something. Redwood an' George hates Big Bill like poison. I personally knows that it was all framed between 'em, if they got to where the treasure was, to bump Big Bill off an' divide between themselves an' me!"

This was news indeed, and Uncle Eb and the boys could not help but register surprise at its telling.

"They'll probably think that room they're in has got all the treasure, too," speculated Giggles. "Gee, Tiny, wasn't it a tough break you had to come along with us? Think what you may be missing?"

The reaction of the dwarf to this sally was not at all as expected. Tiny Thumb took the quip in full seriousness and was quick with his reply.

"You ain't heard me kick, has you? You boys has treated me mighty white for all I've tried to do.

But I just had to show fight when I thought you was all going to get catched again, because if Big Bill ever found out I'd been laying down, he'd of just about . . . well . . . there's no telling what he'd of done. I'm just as scared of that bird as that old boy (pointing at Uncle Eb) says he's afraid of his gran'father!"

"Then you've really come over on our side now?" asked Giggles.

"You said it!" snapped Tiny Thumb, in his high pitched voice. "An' darn glad to be here!"

"Well, we're not!" rejoined Bing, with spirit. "The only side we want to be on is the outside!"

"You figure a way for us to get out, Tiny, and maybe we'll believe you're a friend of ours," challenged Curly, with a wink at the others.

The dwarf turned his back and paced away, mumbling. He approached the pile of débris and climbed carefully over the scattered rocks which sealed the entrance. For minutes the chums sat, unmoving, watching him. There seemed so little any one could do. Each, although not openly admitting the fact, was in the first stages of despair. Here was a situation that for once appeared insurmountable. While there had been the slightest chance of their relying upon their own resources the chums had maintained a sturdy degree of confidence. But of what avail was any human thing they could think of to do now? They were at the mercy of the elements. Old Ebenezer Beecher had craftily arranged for the unsee-

ing, unfeeling rocks to come thundering down should
any one's curiosity be intrigued by the beam, which
he knew it would. And the rocks, once down, con-
stituted the elements that silently, impassively, dis-
puted the rights of these five human beings to life
and liberty. They might cry out and throw themselves down in supplication before the mound of
earth and boulders which filled the entrance, but the
mound would remain unheeding. Oh, it all was so
futile—so terribly and alarmingly hopeless! Even
Spot, the dog, seemed to sense the utter awfulness
of the predicament for he began a sudden, inexplain-
able whimpering and wailing which neither the boys
nor Uncle Eb could stop. And this whimpering only
served to add to the unbearableness of the whole
situation.

"Boys!"

Tiny Thumb's cry caused Uncle Eb and the three
chums to jump nervously.

"I've found a hole in the floor!"

"What!"

The dwarf was instantly surrounded. In the poor
light the boys observed a depression, half covered
by rocks and earth, at the side of the entrance. The
opening was on a slant which seemed to lead back,
under the floor, to the room through which they had
come. Feverishly the boys and Uncle Eb fell to
clawing with their hands to clear away as much of
the débris as they could. But the finish of their
work brought exclamations of disappointment when

it was found that the hole was not large enough to permit of any one getting through it . . . that is, any one save Tiny Thumb!

"What do you suppose is down there?" queried Curly.

"It's as near the spot where the treasure's supposed to be as one could get!" informed Giggles, after a calculating glance at the map on Curly's shirt back. "But, darn it . . . what's the treasure mean to us now?"

"Maybe, if Tiny could get through that hole, he might find a way out and be able to go and bring help," suggested Bing.

"That's just what I was thinking. Tiny, can't we get you through that narrow place?"

The dwarf sized up the hole debatingly. It was obvious that he did not like the idea.

"It's pitch dark down there!" he protested.

"Here's matches," offered Giggles. "We'll see if we can get you through. . . . If we can, you look around down there. And tell us what you see. It looks right now like our only possible chance!"

"All right," consented Tiny Thumb. "But go easy. It's going to be a tight fit. Say—what if you'd get me down there and I couldn't get back up?"

"This isn't any time to worry about 'ifs'," rejoined Giggles. "Come on . . . here you go!"

Giggles and Bing laid hold of the dwarf and pressed him, feet first, into the opening.

"Hands over your head!" ordered Giggles. "You'll never make it with 'em at your sides. . . . That's the stuff! Wait a minute, Bing. His stomach's caught!"

"I—I'm too fat!" gasped Tiny Thumb, wriggling.

"You drank too much water," advised Curly.

"Ouch! . . . Oh, boys!"

"There you are. You're through. Feet touching anything? We don't want to let go your hands unless you've got something to step on."

"Why I . . . I guess so. I feel something. Can you let me down just a little farther? There . . . I . . . all right . . . let go!"

Hearts pounding with hope, the chums and Uncle Eb bent over the hole, all trying to peer down at once.

"Whew . . . smells musty down here! . . . Whew!"

"Light a match . . . !"

"That's what I'm trying to do, believe me!"

The ones above could hear Tiny Thumb as he nervously struck a match against the metal matchbox. They saw the streak of phosphorous as it gleamed several times before the ignition came. Then a slender flame and a startled cry from the dwarf who dropped the match in a panic.

"Christopher! Let me out of here. Take me up, boys! Take me up! Quick!"

"What's the matter?"

"I—I'm standing on a skeleton! That's what's the matter!"

At this information, Uncle Eb scrambled to his feet and backed away, horror-stricken.

"I know what that is. I know what that is! It's that old Indian my grandfather buried. We're done for now! We're done for!"

"Let me up!" pleaded the dwarf, "let me up!"

"Keep still!" yelled Giggles. "Keep still, both of you! Strike another match, Tiny. That skeleton isn't going to hurt you and you're not going to get up till you've looked around down there. We've got to get out of this place, do you realize that? *We* don't want to be skeletons!"

"Let me up! I don't never want to see that thing again!"

"Gee whiz, Giggles, let the poor bird up," cried Curly, his sympathy getting the better of him.

"Nothing doing! If one of us could get down there it would be different . . . but not when he's our only chance. He's going to stay if he's standing on a thousand skeletons!"

It was ten hysterical minutes before Tiny Thumb could be calmed down enough to strike another match. But he finally did, and though the hand which held the match wavered so that the light soon went out, the dwarf gradually gained control over his shattered nerves. Soon he was venturing away from the opening and the boys were straining their ears for words from him.

"Money!" came his voice. "Sacks of money —gold, silver, paper—money . . . money . . . money! You'd think you was in the U. S. Treasury! An', oh Christopher, more skeletons! A whole row of 'em, hanging to the wall. An' a sign up over their heads which says 'This Is What Happens To Those Who Get Too Wise. E.B.' I'm just about under the middle part of the floor in the other room now. Looks like there's a big place right over my head which has been opened to let all this stuff down, an' then closed up again. I don't find no place to get out—not a place. I only got three matches left. What am I going to do?"

"Come back," ordered Giggles, "if you're sure— positive—there's no possible place you might get out!"

The dwarf came back, just reaching the opening as his last match flickered out. He stretched his arms over his head and Giggles and Bing, leaning down, felt about until they secured a grasp on Tiny Thumb's wrists, yanking him up through the hole.

"Tiny, you're all right," complimented Giggles, as the dwarf—now that his ordeal was over—sank down tremblingly, in nervous exhaustion.

"I ought to be if I ain't," was the dwarf's sarcastic retort.

A strained silence fell over the group, a sort of melancholy silence. Even the discovery of the treasure stronghold had not served to arouse their spirits, except as it had held out the hope of escape. Or-

dinarily the finding of this great hoarded wealth
would have provided the boys with their greatest
thrill. It was surprising, though, how little the
achievement in locating the treasure meant when
their present plight was considered. Bags of gold?
Who among them would not surrender all rights to
these bags to any power that might deliver them
from the cave, safe and sound?

"All we can do is keep on hoping," mumbled
Bing, finally.

"What we want to do is to keep on *thinking!*"
insisted Giggles. "I'm frank to say that I don't
place any reliance upon any outside force getting to
us in time."

"But what can *we* do?" asked Curly, helplessly.
"If we only had shovels and picks we might at least
improve our time by trying to make some impression
on that rock pile. But we're not equipped. . . ."

"E.B.'s got us!" moaned Uncle Eb, head in hands.
"E.B.'s got us! Ha! Ha! Ha! Ha! I might a
knowed it! My father said I'd never get away from
him. Never!"

Spot's whimpering raised in scale.

"Shut up!" snapped Giggles, his own nerves on
edge. "That isn't doing anybody any good. It's
just making things harder—so none of us can think
. . . or . . . or try to do anything. Shut up!"

Uncle Eb restrained himself with an effort, rocking back and forth in hysterical fashion, pulling
at his whiskers with gnarled fingers. Giggles got

up and walked over to the pool of water, looking
down into it, studyingly. He was facing west, as he
knew, for the bluff faced west. Beyond that wall of
rock—that under-the-water ledge—Lake Michigan
no doubt stretched her mighty body. Either that
or there was another section of the underground
cave. But this was improbable for it would hardly
have permitted the sunlight to have crept in this far.
And Giggles could tell, from the lights and shadows
in the water, that the sun must be striking the outer
face of the bluff at a sharp angle now. He glanced
at his wrist watch. Three o'clock! In a little more
than two hours the sun would be down close to the
horizon. Already the shadows in the water were
lengthening. Daylight was beginning to recede.
The half glow in the room would retreat, leaving
them all in darkness—a darkness which would persist
until close to noon of the following day, until the sun
was high in the heavens. Cloudy weather would
mean scarcely any light at all. This would make
their confinement in the cave even more horrible.
The longer they were forced to remain the less
morale they would be able to hold. And finally,
weak and desperate, Giggles could picture wild
scenes, maddening acts, doings that none of them
would be capable of in their right senses. The
thought came to him of the feeling which must have
possessed men trapped in a submarine at sea, or
of miners caught below ground, awaiting the end.
His heart gave some frantic leaps. Giggles stiff-

ened, clenching his fists. This would never do! If a fellow lost his nerve even the slightest hope, the vaguest chance would be gone. He mustn't let himself think of the consequences or the folks at home. He mustn't!

As Giggles gazed below, his attention was suddenly caught by sight of a large fish which came finning majestically under the ledge from the outside world.

"Fellows, look here!"

A second bidding was unnecessary. Bing and Curly and Uncle Eb and Tiny Thumb made a scramble for the edge of the pool.

"Don't I wish I was him!" exclaimed Curly, wistfully.

"Me, too!" joined in Bing.

"Say!" exclaimed Giggles, "there's an idea. A whale of an idea. Why not? The way out of here is by water!"

The four others stared at one another, uncomprehending.

"How . . . by giving the fish a message to deliver?" asked Curly, with attempted lightness.

"No! Listen—I'm not joshing this time. I'm in earnest. Don't know why I didn't think of this before—or you fellows either, for that matter!"

"What is it?"

"Don't you remember what we used to do?" Giggles was tremendously excited. "The stunt we'd pull when we were in swimming by the old dock at Bean Blossom?"

"Oh, you mean taking a big weight or boat anchor and jumping off the dock and letting the weight carry us to the bottom; and walking along under water—under the dock—then letting go the weight and shooting to the top?"

"That's it!"

Bing and Curly glanced down at the water, surveying the depth at which the ledge extended under the surface and the probable depth of the water itself. Then they shook their heads.

"Good idea but it can't be done here. Ledge is too far down, water too deep. Besides, you don't know how thick that ledge is through. It might be too far for you, and you'd drown!"

"I've already thought of all those objections," persisted Giggles. "But when you're in the fix we're in anything that has a chance is worth trying!"

Giggles began pulling determinedly at his shirt. Bing and Curly caught their chum and forcibly held him.

"Not so fast! Are you crazy? Let's think this thing over. You're not going to jump right in and risk your life that way!"

"It's no use. E.B.'s got us!" muttered Uncle Eb, gloomily.

"Besides, if this stunt was worth trying," argued Bing, "we ought to draw cuts to see which one should try it. It's not fair to—!"

"That's right !" insisted the dwarf, to the chums' surprise.

"Can *you* swim?" asked Curly.

"Sure!" answered the dwarf, proudly.

"Well," objected Curly, interposing a further thought on the matter, "there's no sense in any of us taking such a risk as this unless it was as the very last resort. We'd want to wait several days at least as we're in no immediate danger of dying. And we might be rescued in that length of time !"

Giggles shook his head.

"I don't agree with you," he said. "If any one's going to attempt this hazard, he must do it when he's at his fullest strength. This is no stunt for a weakling. In a couple of days we'll have noticed the loss of food and our chances would be less of making it, if it can be made. Besides, our nerves won't be as good. You all know that. And nerve counts, too! No, sir! If I was elected to undertake this, I'd want to tackle it as soon as possible or leave it alone. As for the chances of our being rescued in several days . . . well, all I say is—give me this chance !"

Bing and Curly hesitated, undecided. Their better judgment told them that Giggles was probably right in every particular although it was exceedingly difficult to determine what should be done.

"If you did get out," speculated Bing, "you'd have a long swim of it to get ashore . . . and you'd probably be exhausted when you came to the top!"

"That's all in the chance," grinned Giggles.

"Well, whoever takes it, the chance is going to be drawn for," said Curly, resolutely.

"No it isn't!" declared Giggles. "This isn't any time for jockeying. And it isn't any time for undue modesty, either. You fellows know I'm the best swimmer and that, everything considered, I ought to have the best chances of coming through. That's the deciding point right there."

"Well, I . . . we . . . no it isn't!"

"You know it is! I appreciate your offers and all that. And I know either one of you would be game to try if it fell to your lot."

"You're forgetting me!" objected Tiny Thumb, with a trace of indignation. "Why don't you let me try it first?"

Giggles looked down upon the earnest little pygmy man and placed a hand on his head.

"Tiny, you're sure doing your best to make things up to us," he said. "But you're too small. You'd go down all right, but your legs are too short. When it came to running along bottom you'd be out of luck."

Giggles commenced again to remove his clothes, bending down to untie his shoes.

"It'll be dark in a couple of hours," he said. "The light's as good now as it'll ever be. If it looks like I've made it, that is, if I haven't come up on this side of the ledge again you fellows wait three days. Anybody from outside ought to reach you in that time if I lead 'em to where you are. If they don't . . . well . . . then maybe you'll want to try what I'm going to try now!"

Giggles was stripped to his B.V.D.'s. Bing and Curly watched their chum, feeling the blood pump through their veins excitedly. Uncle Eb, the most hysterical of all, burst into hoarse sobs. Spot leaped up to lick the tears away. Tiny Thumb showed his disgust of this scene by turning his back on it.

"You'll never make it!" cried Uncle Eb. "You'll never make it! E.B.'s got us! E.B.'s——!"

"Don't do it, Giggles, don't do it!" begged Bing and Curly, affected by the old hermit's outburst. "If something happened to you and then we got out we'd never forgive ourselves!"

"Tee, hee, hee!" giggled Giggles. "That works both ways. If I stayed here and then we didn't get out, I'd never forgive myself for not having gone! Come on, now. Help me find a nice big stone that I can lay hold of and take down with me!"

The chums looked about, dazedly, passing from rock to rock. Finally a stone was uncovered about the size that Giggles could carry in comfort after it was placed in his arms.

"She's sure heavy," was Giggles verdict. "Should take me to the bottom like a shot! Help me carry her over to the edge."

This done, Giggles turned to Curly.

"All right, pal, now you can take your shirt off. I want to wear it. If I get out, that map on the back might help me locate you fellows again, if it doesn't wash off!"

Curly peeled his shirt, holding it up to take a look at Giggles' drawing before passing it over.

"I don't see how you figured anything out from that," he said.

"I don't either, now," admitted Giggles. "It certainly looks sick off your back! Well, old shirt, you'll have a great 'tail' to tell if we come through all right, won't you?"

Tiny Thumb grinned at this and shook his head in admiration of the youth who was purposely making light of the great risk he was so soon to undergo.

Giggles turned impulsively upon Curly, unattaching his wrist watch.

"Here, I'll make you a present of this trusty old ticker," he said.

"Thanks," Curly replied, taking the watch and strapping it to his own wrist. "You're generous all of a sudden!"

"No, I'm not!" insisted Giggles. "I'll want it back when I see you again!"

Curly did not have the heart to reply to this. As if sensing his chums' pessimistic thought, Giggles swung about toward the pool.

"Excuse me a minute. I'm going to dive in and get accustomed to the water!"

A splash followed Giggles' words and the chums, from the edge, saw his body go flashing down in a white arch. Giggles soon came to the top, treaded water and blew up a little spout, playfully.

"How is she?" called Bing.

"Not bad! Where'd that fish go?"

"He scooted for the other side!"

"What? Well, the poor sport! Wait till I catch him!"

Giggles pulled himself out of the water and crawled back on the rocky edge, helped by Bing and Curly. He ran over to slap Uncle Eb on the back and pet the whimpering Spot.

"A great pair, you are!" he chided. "I'm ashamed of you, Uncle. Honest, I am. You're brave one minute and all to pieces the next!"

"Uncle Eb don't mean to be this way," apologized the old hermit. "It's E.B. He's the one . . . !"

Giggles retraced his dripping steps to the edge of the pool. He was having a battle with his inner self and he wanted to hasten his attempt before his nerve was sapped. A little voice was trying to say to him, "You can't ever make it! You can't ever make it!" And Giggles was calling upon all the will power he possessed to overcome it. "I can! I can!" he kept answering. But the little voice was growing stronger every moment. Uncle Eb's despondency had seemed to join with it. "See, he thinks you're a goner!" the voice suggested. "And you *are* a goner! You can't ever!" "I CAN and I WILL!" Giggles fairly shouted to himself, as he knelt, heart thumping so that he could feel it against his ear drums, and prepared to lift the stone.

"Giggles, you shouldn't do this!" Curly cried out, with involuntary frenzy.

"Lay that stone across my knees till I get my arms around it," ordered Giggles, quietly. "Now face me around so I'm looking at the ledge. . . . There! That's fine! Now if I can't keep my grip on this rock I'll have to come up and try it again."

Bing and Curly found the corners of their mouths twitching and eyes growing moist. The dwarf stood nearby, his little face a mass of worried wrinkles.

"You—you're the gamest fellow I ever seen!" said Tiny Thumb, in his high pitched voice.

"Cut it!" ordered Giggles. "And I don't want any good-bys, either! I'm going to *make* this, understand? I'll bring help just as soon as I can. Hang on till I get back!"

Giggles drew a mighty breath and practiced holding it. He drew several more. Then, almost before those watching were aware of his movement, he had side-stepped and dropped in!

The waters closed over Giggles' head in a churning splash and for a moment it was impossible to see. Uncle Eb, crawling to the edge on hands and knees, bent over to peer after the intrepid Giggles, moaning the while. Spot cringed beside his master, hanging his paws over the edge and blinking at the disturbed surface of the water.

"There he is!" cried Bing, after an anxious moment which seemed several eternities long. "He's just touching bottom! He's in a crouched position . . . see! He's straightening up a little. Look at him strain against the weight of the water! He can hardly stay down. It's a fight. See the bubbles! He's letting his breath out to decrease his buoyancy. He's almost under the ledge . . . there he goes . . . out of sight . . . !"

"He's gone!" gasped the watchers. "GONE!"

CHAPTER XV

AGONIZING SUSPENSE

JIM McCLEERY and Samuel Nevens were two of Bean Blossom's most prominent fishermen. It was really the only claim they had to distinction and they made the most of it by continually seeking out new haunts where scaly dwellers of the crystal deep might repose. Perhaps coincidence played a small part in the fact of these two fisher folk being in a particular position on a particular sunny afternoon at the particularly particular moment of thirteen minutes to four o'clock. At any rate, trolling peacefully along as they were, Jim McCleery and Samuel Nevens were totally unprepared for the startling phenomenon which was so shortly to present itself. Jim McCleery was taking his turn at rowing and Sam was in the stern, paying out the line.

"Looks like along this bluff ought to be a great place," Jim had just gotten through remarking. "Funny we never thought of trying it here before. You should get a strike, sure!"

"Deep as the mischief, too!" answered Sam.

And then the startling phenomena occurred. Between the boat and the bluff a something shot to the surface, made a gulping gasp, turned over and sunk again . . . slowly . . . turning over as it do so.

Sam was so startled that he almost fell out of the boat. Jim, hearing the splash, glanced over the side just in time to catch a glimpse of something white, struggling weakly, spasmodically, under water!

"What in tarnation?"

"It's a boy!" yelled Sam, and forthwith dove out of the boat with his clothes on.

Jim, convinced that Sam had gone loony, backed water frantically with his oars and strove to keep the boat in position near the spot where his companion had disappeared.

"Boy?" said Jim to himself. "Boy! How could a boy come bobbing up out of the water? . . . Maybe he said '*buoy*.' That's it—buoy! The darn fool's dove in after a buoy!"

But if Jim didn't yet know what it was all about, Sam did. He had to go twelve feet under water to reach the fellow clad in the B.V.D.'s and the shirt, but he clutched the inert form from behind and struck out for the top, fighting mightily with his burden.

Jim's eyes bulged as Sam appeared with his arm about a human figure. He stuck out an oar which Sam grabbed and the next few minutes were strenuous ones for both men as they lifted the body over the gunwale of the boat.

"Row!" sputtered Sam, giving all his attention to the unconscious youth. "Row for all you're worth to Bailey's Landing!"

"Jiminy, that's Al Hungerford's son, ain't it?"

"Row!" reiterated Sam, starting to work at re-suscitation. "Yep, that's who it is! We've got to get him ashore quick!"

As Jim bent to the oars, the line in the stern of the boat began to sing.

"Good night!" he exclaimed, excitedly. "There's another fish!"

"We should worry about that one," said Sam, grimly. "It's this *white* fish that I'm concerned about!"

Bailey's Landing was a good mile distant but it is highly probable that no better time was ever turned in for that distance than Jim McCleery did on that particularly particular summer afternoon. Before the boat docked, those on shore were apprised that something unusual had happened by the yells from the two fishermen. And eager hands lifted the boy from the boat while curious ears picked up the un-believable story of the rescue.

"Don't ask me to explain it!" protested Jim McCleery, "she's all beyond me!"

"Did he dive off the cliff?"

"If he did I didn't hear him splash. And what would a boy be diving off a cliff that high for? Be-sides, did you see those funny lines on the back of his shirt?"

"He's coming around, I think," said Sam, as the form was stretched out on the dock. "He'd shipped

219

considerable water. He groaned once on the way in. Anybody got a car here?"

"Corky Pierce has," volunteered some one.

"Soon as he comes to we ought to rush him into town. Looks like the boy'll be pretty sick for a few hours."

"How about a doctor?"

"He can't do no more than we can for the time being. We'll have him to a doctor as soon as one could get out here."

Twenty minutes work over Giggles served to restore him to consciousness. But Giggles, as Sam had predicted, was a thoroughly miserable boy and hardly aware of what was happening around him. He did, however, further mystify those attending him, by what appeared to be the wildest of utterances.

"Bing! Curly! The cave! Oh, don't do that! You're hurting me! Oh! The cave! Get help! They're trapped!"

"Who's trapped? What cave?"

"Under Uncle Eb's house, you know! The beam! I did it! Get them out! They're trapped, I tell you . . . trapped!"

"Let the boy alone!" ordered Sam. "He don't know what he's saying yet. He's thinking of everybody he ever knew. And cave? He's clean nutty!"

It was not until Giggles had been rushed the remaining six miles in to Bean Blossom, against his protest, and carried up to Doc Moore's office with a wondering crowd following him, that the half-drowned boy was able to impress upon those closest to him the stern reality of his previous jabberings. His depiction of the three desperate characters brought Constable Stricler on the run. The constable quickly deputized five men and gave them arms. A gang of workers on the county road, just quitting for the day, were picked up in a truck and started pell mell for the region of the bluff, taking along shovels and all equipment for digging, including dynamite, should it be found necessary to blast. The parents of the three boys were notified and the three fathers joined with other citizens in starting out for the scene of the mad doings. Quite the biggest sensation, however, was the news of the great underground cave. Giggles had been wise enough to keep mum on the treasure part of the story, divulging only such facts as concerned those in danger. While Bean Blossom was turning itself upside down and the town was fast depopulating in favor of Uncle Eb's premises, Giggles was being forcibly detained in Doc Moore's office, it requiring three good-sized men to keep him from breaking away.

"Let me go! Let me go!" Giggles cried. "I'm all right. I know what I'm doing! They can't ever find the place unless I go along. You've got to take me out there. What did you do with that shirt I was wearing? You threw it away? . . . Where'd you throw it? What do you mean, doing a thing like that? Go get it! I got to have it . . . it's valuable!"

"For Pete's sake, some one fetch the lad's shirt for him before he goes bughouse for good!" intreated poor Sam Nevens, who had borne the burden of caring for Giggles since the Bean Blossom youth had bobbed up, in such astounding fashion, from the depths of the lake.

The much abused shirt was fortunately retrieved from the doctor's waste basket and Giggles spread it out anxiously to view the condition of his drawings on the back. He exclaimed with joy as he found the markings still discernible. Grabbing up a piece of cardboard, Giggles slipped it inside the wet shirt so that the cloth could be smoothed out against it.

"See—here's the map of the cave. You can't read it . . . but I can! I can lead anybody to where the fellows are, in half an hour. I told Bing and Curly I'd be back for 'em if I got out safe and I'm going to keep my word. Let me out of here!"

Doc Moore looked at the determined youth and shrugged his shoulders helplessly.

"Let him go," he finally said to Giggles' captors. "The boy will do himself more harm raving like that than he will going back to the cave and searching for his chums!"

Five minutes later, Sam escorted the youth he had saved from drowning out to a waiting automobile and the two were sent racing after the mob which had already left.

222

The house on the bluff set a good quarter of a mile back from the nearest road, but a genuine path was certainly beaten to it this late afternoon in summer. Dusk fell on premises, hitherto forbidden territory, jammed with human forms and more arriving each minute. The entire countryside was aroused and telegraph keys had begun their clicking. The world would hear about this! News of a possible treasure had trekked out, too, and every Bean Blossom resident was piecing together with his neighbor all that he had ever heard about the queer old Uncle Eb and his eccentric grandfather, Ebenezer Beecher. It was highly possible, indeed quite probable, in the light of these developments, that Ebenezer Beecher had been a tyrannical pirate of early days, raiding unprotected settlements with the aid of outlaw Indians and other hardy characters. Oh, he was a black-dyed villain, that fellow! And to think that it had fallen to the lot of three Bean Blossom youths —Giggles, Bing and Curly—to have unearthed this tremendous sensation. They would be the talk, yes, the idol of the town for months and years to come!

Giggles was forced to fight his way into Uncle Eb's house, so great was the crowd which milled about him. There were cheers at sight of him and lanterns flashed on his face. But Giggles was mindful only of his chums and what he might be able to do for them. He went below quickly, as Constable Stricler hurried out to see that a stronger guard was placed about the house. It would not do to have any undesirables pushing inside.

Giggles came upon the workers and the special deputies, gathered in the first room of the cave, under the basement, uncertain how to proceed, exactly as Giggles had anticipated.

"Gee, this is a much bigger cave than we counted on!" said one.

And Giggles could tell that the men were rather awed, just as he and his chums had been.

Consulting the markings on the shirt from time to time, Giggles led the way swiftly, organizing the expedition of rescuers by directing that the deputies go ahead to intercept the white chieftain, the colored giant and the Indian if this trio had not already effected their escape.

"Watch out for that bunch!" Giggles warned. "They're armed and they may shoot!"

It was now close to seven o'clock and the cave was even darker if this could have been possible. But there were many lanterns and flashlights with the party and these turned the darkness into a day which revealed much more of the cavernous interior than Giggles had ever seen before. The sight was one of such indescribable grandeur that the men were kept in one constant state of Oh's and Ah's.

As Giggles passed some of the places which already, to him, had become landmarks, he could not suppress a peculiar, tingling feeling. How much had happened in the last twenty-four hours! Seven o'clock the night before he and Bing and Curly had been blissfully ignorant of all the tempestuous happenings which were just ahead of them. Perhaps it had been a good thing. Such an adventure as they had been through was one to take as it had come, rather than to have considered in advance. Certainly they would never have entered upon such a thrilling succession of events had they been able to picture them prior to starting out. But, now that they were about at an end, and Giggles felt reasonably sure that his chums and Uncle Eb and Tiny Thumb would be rescued from their entombment, he took a savage joy in the thought of the experience which had been theirs.

"Look out, now!" he advised the deputies, as he started them ahead through the passageway which led to the first treasure room. "In here's where you may find the fellows I was telling you about!"

Sure enough!

Big Bill, the white chieftain; George, the colored giant; and Redwood, the Indian, were found. But such a sorry plight as each of them was in! Battered and bruised and broken, the three lay about the room. Big Bill was sprawled flat on his back inside a half-filled chest, his arms dangling over the sides, a big gash on his head . . . his shirt front bloody. George was sitting moaning in a corner with an arm hanging useless at his side and the side of his face badly lacerated. Redwood was crumpled face downward on the floor with a bullet wound in his thigh and a gold necklace gripped in his fingers. All three were alive, the colored giant being the only one who knew it at that moment, however. Giggles remembered then, what Tiny Thumb had said about how George and Redwood had hated the white chieftain, and it was not hard for Giggles to visualize the glorious battle which had ensued when the three had thought they had stumbled upon the treasure. Evidently Big Bill had been quite some match for his two burly opponents. The charred remains of a torch gave indication of its having burned for some time after the riotous conflict had taken place.

"Golly," said Giggles to himself, "by the way those boys look, they might as well have been caught in that cave-in!"

The road workers, upon investigation, found that the ceiling over the passageway had not broken down except over the entrance to the room in which the two chums, the old hermit and the dwarf were held captive. This accounted for the fact that the pursuing trio escaped unscathed, although the débris had piled into the passage for some distance. A squad of diggers immediately set to work, throwing aside the loose dirt and fragments, preparatory to getting down to the big boulders which formed the most formidable barrier.

Inside the room, sitting in pitch darkness, huddled together for comfort and companionship, Bing, Curly, Uncle Eb, and Tiny Thumb speculated over and over again on whether Giggles had reached the outside in safety. It was Uncle Eb's gloomy opinion that Giggles had failed; the cliff wall had been too thick; he had been unable to clear it; then, powerless to hold his breath longer, he had been strangled in the water and sucked out into the lake. Tiny Thumb refused to voice an opinion only to mutter that he should have been the one to have made the try and not Giggles. Bing and Curly hoped against hope. They had quieted down somewhat, as had Uncle Eb and Spot, but the calm which had come over them was more a calm of nerve exhaustion than of nerve control. The least little imaginary noise startled them almost out of their wits so that they were clutching each other in an instant. A sudden inexplicable ripple of water as it eddied under the ledge, struck cold fear in their hearts. There were even sights to be seen in the darkness—sights which had a creepy way of vanishing when hands were rubbed over eyes. So, with all these unreal impressions, the sudden reverberating of a dull boom which caused the room in which they were sitting to tremble violently, sent the four into a mild state of hysterics.

"What was that?"

"Did—did you feel anything?"

"The . . . the earth shook . . . or was I dreaming?"

"Maybe there's a thunder storm out. I heard a sort of rumble!"

Fifteen more minutes. It was four minutes to two in the morning now. Fifteen more minutes and another boom, followed by a scattered falling of rock particles.

"Hurrah!" cried Bing, embracing Curly. "Somebody's getting to us. That was a blast! We're being rescued!"

Soon a pin-pointed ray of light seeped through and the sound of shovel blades could be heard plainly. There were shouts from outside . . . and . . . Giggles' voice!

"Hello, in there. Are you all right?"

"Fine!" shouted all four, with an enthusiasm born of intense relief.

A few dragging minutes elapsed ere the passage could be cleared enough to permit entrance or exit. Then the tired Giggles bounded through to meet a pair of tired buddies and an equally tired Uncle Eb and Tiny Thumb, not forgetting Spot, the dog. But all were happy, oh . . . so happy!

"I'm putting a guard over this treasure," Constable Stricler informed Uncle Eb. "And I'm considering the treasure your property until it's proven otherwise—which I don't suppose it will be."

"Well, not until I make my will anyhow," said Uncle Eb. "If this here all belongs to me, I'm a makin' it known afore all ye folks that my property goes to these three boys. They's sure deservin' of it and I'm a goin' to be glad to git rid of most of it, believe you me! I didn't never expect to see the outside of this here cave agin!"

"The first thing for all you birds to think about is going home and getting about twenty-four hours' good sleep," reminded the constable. "This cave's going to be here when you wake up, and so's the treasure. It'll be several weeks anyhow before you have any idea of how much the treasure's worth but from what you tell me I shouldn't be surprised if it runs up into the thousands—perhaps several hundred of 'em at least. All of which oughtn't to put any gray hairs on your heads!"

"Well . . . well . . . what about *me?*" asked Tiny Thumb, feeling considerably left out and just a bit concerned about his disposition.

"You were with that other gang, weren't you?" demanded the constable. "And they're goin' to jail as quick as I can get 'em there!"

"He *was* with the other gang," Giggles put in quickly, "but we converted him, constable. And he helped us out considerable, too—locating the treasure. Seems to me like he's entitled to a reward. Say—if you don't mind, and if he doesn't either, we'd like to kind of adopt him. Maybe there'll be something for him to do in Bean Blossom, unless he'd rather follow the circus!"

But from the way the dwarf spread the wrinkles over his face in an appreciative grin, it was evident that Giggles' suggestion met with unanimous approval.

"What are we going to do with our share of the treasure when we get it?" asked Curly, some moments later, when the chums were by themselves.

"There you go!" joshed Bing. "Counting your pennies before they're coined!"

"Well, you heard what Uncle Eb said," defended Curly, the freckles on his face turning a deep red, "and I *do* think we're entitled to . . . !"

"Of course we are!" supported Giggles. "And I don't have any question but what there's going to be plenty of treasure to go around. At the risk of being previous I'm herewith announcing that whatever treasure comes to me is going to be turned into a college education!"

Bing and Curly looked at one another approvingly.

"Good!" voiced Curly. "That solves about our last problem. Only I think we ought to agree right now to all go to the same college so we can all be in on anything else exciting that one of us might stir up!"

"That's taken by consent!" announced Bing, warmly.

"As for excitement," added Giggles, when he, with his two chums, had climbed into his father's car ready for the trip back to town, "there's lots of mysterious things we haven't cleared up yet about this cave. We've still got a lot of exploring and figuring to do!"

"Well—all I've got to say is—there's not going

to be any more figuring on another shirt of mine!" declared Curly.

"Can you beat that?" exploded Giggles, turning to Bing as though offended. "And after I *washed* it for him, too!"

[(1)]

THE END

This Isn't All!

Would you like to know what became of the good friends you have made in this book?

Would you like to read other stories continuing their adventures and experiences, or other books quite as entertaining by the same author?

On the *reverse side* of the wrapper which comes with this book, you will find a wonderful list of stories which you can buy at the same store where you got this book.

Don't throw away the Wrapper

Use it as a handy catalog of the books you want some day to have. But in case you do mislay it, write to the Publishers for a complete catalog.

STORIES OF SPORT AND ADVENTURE

By HAROLD M. SHERMAN

May be had wherever books are sold. Ask for Grosset & Dunlap's list

The Home Run Series

Here are thrilling baseball stories filled with fast playing and keen rivalry. The author of these books writes from his own experience as a player.

BASES FULL!   SAFE!

HIT BY PITCHER   HIT AND RUN

Rousing Football Stories

These stories of the gridiron are packed full of excitement and real smashing, heart-breaking football.

HOLD THAT LINE!   BLOCK THAT KICK!

TOUCHDOWN!   FIGHT 'EM, BIG THREE!

ONE MINUTE TO PLAY

The Fighting Five Basketball Series

These stories record the uphill fight of a group of boys to rouse the citizens of a dull town by winning a championship against great odds.

MAYFIELD'S FIGHTING FIVE

GET 'EM, MAYFIELD

Other Stories of Sport and Adventure

BEYOND THE DOG'S NOSE   FLASHING STEEL

DON RADER, TRAIL BLAZER   DING PALMER, AIR DETECTIVE

NUMBER 44   FLYING HEELS

CAMERON MacBAIN, BACKWOODSMAN

A story of American Junior League Baseball

BATTER UP!

GROSSET & DUNLAP, Publishers, NEW YORK

THE REX LEE FLYING STORIES
By THOMSON BURTIS

Individual Colored Wrappers. Illustrated. Every Volume Complete in Itself.

May be had wherever books are sold. Ask for Grosset & Dunlap's list.

The author of this series of exciting flying stories is an experienced aviator. He says, "During my five years in the army I performed nearly every sort of flying duty—instructor, test pilot, bombing, photographing pilot, etc., in every variety of ship, from tiny scout planes to the gigantic three-motored Italian Caproni."

Not only has this author had many experiences as a flyer; a list of his activities while knocking around the country includes postal clerk, hobo, actor, writer, mutton chop salesman, preacher, roughneck in the oil fields, newspaper man, flyer, scenario writer in Hollywood and synthetic clown with the Sells Floto Circus. Having lived an active, daring life, and possessing a gift for good story telling, he is well qualified to write these adventures of a red-blooded dare devil young American who became one of the country's greatest flyers.

REX LEE; GYPSY FLIER
REX LEE; ON THE BORDER PATROL
REX LEE; RANGER OF THE SKY
REX LEE; SKY TRAILER
REX LEE; ACE OF THE AIR MAIL
REX LEE; NIGHT FLIER
REX LEE'S MYSTERIOUS FLIGHT

GROSSET & DUNLAP, Publishers, NEW YORK

WESTERN STORIES FOR BOYS

By JAMES CODY FERRIS

Individual Colored Wrappers and Illustrations by
WALTER S. ROGERS
Each Volume Complete in Itself.

Thrilling tales of the great west, told primarily for boys but which will be read by all who love mystery, rapid action, and adventures in the great open spaces.

The Manly Boys, Roy and Teddy, are the sons of an old ranchman, the owner of many thousands of heads of cattle. The lads know how to ride, how to shoot, and how to take care of themselves under any and all circumstances.

The cowboys of the X Bar X Ranch are real cowboys, on the job when required but full of fun and daring—a bunch any reader will be delighted to know.

THE X BAR X BOYS ON THE RANCH
THE X BAR X BOYS IN THUNDER CANYON
THE X BAR X BOYS ON WHIRLPOOL RIVER
THE X BAR X BOYS ON BIG BISON TRAIL
THE X BAR X BOYS AT THE ROUND-UP
THE X BAR X BOYS AT NUGGET CAMP
THE X BAR X BOYS AT RUSTLER'S GAP
THE X BAR X BOYS AT GRIZZLY PASS
THE X BAR X BOYS LOST IN THE ROCKIES

GROSSET & DUNLAP, Publishers, NEW YORK

THE WESTY MARTIN BOOKS

By PERCY KEESE FITZHUGH
Author of the " Tom Slade " and " Roy Blakeley " Books, Etc.

**Individual Colored Wrappers. Illustrated.
Every Volume Complete in Itself.**

May be had wherever books are sold. Ask for Grosset & Dunlap's list

Westy Martin, known to every friend of Roy Blakeley, appears as the hero of adventures quite different from those in which we have seen him participate as a Scout of Bridgeboro and Temple Camp. On his way to the Yellowstone the bigness of the vast West and the thoughts of the wild preserve that he is going to visit make him conscious of his own smallness and the futility of "boy scouting" and woods lore in this great region. Yet he was to learn that if it had not been for his scout training he would never have been able to survive the experiences he had in these stories.

WESTY MARTIN

WESTY MARTIN IN THE YELLOWSTONE

WESTY MARTIN IN THE ROCKIES

WESTY MARTIN ON THE SANTE FE TRAIL

WESTY MARTIN ON THE OLD INDIAN TRAIL

WESTY MARTIN IN THE LAND OF THE PURPLE
    SAGE

GROSSET & DUNLAP, Publishers, NEW YORK